# The Book on Qualified Opportunity Zones

## Second Edition

**A Comprehensive Guide for Investors, Developers, Business Owners and Professional Advisors**

DAVID S. ROSEN

VADIM D. RONZHES

For information regarding permission, please write to:

David S. Rosen
c/o RS&F
405 York Road
Towson, Maryland 21204

**Printed by:**
David Rosen/RS&F

Printed in the United States of America

First Printing Edition, 2022
ISBN 979-8-8064893-2-7

*Table of Contents*

## The Book on Qualified Opportunity Zones
## Second Edition

# About the Authors

## David S. Rosen

David S. Rosen, Esq., CPA is one of the leading tax advisors in the United States and the author of the forthcoming *Family Offices* Portfolio that will be published by Bloomberg Tax. David has led the tax structuring and planning for hundreds of opportunity zone, real estate and business transactions, including some of the largest opportunity zone transactions to date. With a clientele comprising family offices, real estate developers and large closely held businesses, David oversees the tax planning for many of the wealthiest families in the country and their businesses.

## Vadim D. Ronzhes

Vadim Ronzhes is a tax attorney and CPA with over 15 years' experience providing business advisory and structuring for real estate developers and closely held businesses. Vadim has intimate knowledge in dealing with federal and state tax agencies and on compliance matters as an experienced civil and criminal tax litigator.

DAVID ROSEN

VADIM RONZHES

# The Book on Qualified Opportunity Zones

# A Note to Our Readers

The development of the *Book on Qualified Opportunity Zones (Second Edition)* arose following dozens of real-life transactions (many of which have culminated in the creation of qualified opportunity funds that are currently developing real estate and business projects under the program). Over the past four years, we have prepared detailed transaction memos, researched every component of the statute and regulations and developed practical tools for stakeholders. Ultimately, we felt that combining our work into a comprehensive "book" will benefit our team, our clients, and other participants in the new industry focusing on the opportunity zone program.

The key changes in this Second Edition include updating the content to reflect the Final Regulations, analysis of guidance issued during the past 3 years, address new laws and promulgations, and add examples and analysis based on the actual operation of these transactions, as well as restructuring the book into a more accessible format.

To date, the success of the opportunity zone program remains unknown. While it appears that the program is robust and meeting its objectives, we are too early to make any conclusions. One day we will have the facts and data to reflect whether the program met its potential. We always anticipated early deals would consist of shovel ready projects and later deals would incorporate new infrastructure, mass transportation, and municipal incentives in order to invest in some of the neediest communities in the country. Our expectation is that the program will cause billions of dollars of investment into low-income communities that would, in many cases, not be spent in these locations, resulting in substantial improvements to many of the communities that need it the most.

This book is broken out into two parts as follows:

**Part 1 ("General Overview")** sets forth in Chapters 1-4 an overview and background of the qualified opportunity zone program, together with a summary of the tax benefits and the structure of the program, as well as a detailed practical example of the QOZ program for investors, real estate developers and business owners.

**Part 2 ("Analysis for Tax and Legal Professionals")** in Chapters 5-13 provides a comprehensive and detailed analysis of all aspects of the qualified opportunity zone program suitable for tax and real estate professional advisors, equivalent to a complete tax treatise covering §1400Z-1 and §1400Z-2. This tax analysis is the most thorough that has been published on this topic to date.

For many stakeholders in the qualified opportunity zone community, the work is just beginning. To that end, we can assist you to structure your transactions, coordinate with outside advisors and prepare for the ten-year holding period.

Yet, we have learned that much of our work begins after the deal has been closed and the project is (or has been) constructed. Our team has developed an approach to assist funds to comply with the extensive set of rules during the ten-year period. Annual compliance testing is required, and failure can led to the loss of all the expected tax benefits.

Our team is excited about the significant impact we have already had for many opportunity zone projects, large and small, having closed over $10 billion of projects to date. We look forward to many more comparable opportunities. To that end, we believe that RS&F is the ideal accounting firm partner for real estate and venture funds, law firms representing opportunity zone projects, family office investors and business owners that are considering operations in the opportunity zone.

This book is intended as a comprehensive technical resource for tax and real estate professionals, as well as other stakeholders in the Qualified Opportunity Zone ("QOZ") community. This book is not, however, designed to provide specific structuring advice or address topics outside of the scope of the QOZ program (such as partnership or corporate tax matters). The design and structure of a particular project under the QOZ program, and structuring ideas relating to specific project goals should be addressed with our team on a project-specific basis, after we have obtained a thorough understanding of the facts, the tax attributes of the parties and related pertinent information.

To assist our readers, we have included several appendices. We highly recommend that readers familiarize themselves with key terminology. To that end, Appendix A (the "ABCs of OZs") includes a detailed glossary of key terms that will help readers that are not familiar with the QOZ program to understand the terminology, abbreviations and technical items contained in this book. Appendix B provides a sample chronology which provides a straightforward view of the lifecycle of a QOZ investment.

**The authors invite suggested changes, whether substantive or even to point out typos, corrections (or criticism of our cover design or font size). We are not perfect, and have little doubt that the community can find opinions, conclusions or statements that should be corrected. To that end, we encourage the community to provide their own opinions that can be included in future versions of this Book. The views expressed herein reflect the authors' thoughts when initially written and any opinions or conclusions are subject to change.**

**DISCLAIMER: Before using any information contained in these materials, a taxpayer should seek advice based on the taxpayer's particular circumstances from an independent tax advisor. Tax advisors should research these issues independently rather than rely on these materials. This book is a reference for educational use for the community and should not be relied upon without independent verification of the underlying law.**

Please do not hesitate to contact our team to assist you or your clients with an opportunity zone project. We have gone deeper than virtually any group in the entire country and would love to share our hard work with you.

**David S. Rosen, Esq., CPA**
**Vadim D. Ronzhes, CPA, Esq.**
**Rosen, Sapperstein & Friedlander LLC**
**405 York Road**
**Towson, MD 21204**
**(410) 581-0800**

# Part 1

# General Overview

# CHAPTER ONE

# Overview and Background of Qualified Opportunity Zones

## BACKGROUND OF THE OPPORTUNITY ZONE LEGISLATION

The 2017 tax reform legislation (which is commonly referred to as the Tax Cut and Jobs Act of 2017 or the "TCJA") created one of the most ambitious tax incentive programs in modern history: *Qualified Opportunity Zones*.[1] The qualified opportunity zone program is based on the bipartisan "Investing in Opportunity Act" originally introduced in the House of Representatives and separately in the Senate in February 2017 with the support of dozens of Republicans and Democrats.[2] The original concept behind the program is credited to a white paper from April 2015 issued by the Economic Innovation Group ("EIG") entitled "Unlocking

Private Capital to Facilitate Economic Growth in Distressed Areas".[3] Prominent supporters of the legislation include Senator Tim Scott (R) of South Carolina and Senator Cory Booker (D) of New Jersey (both of whom were sponsors of the Senate version of the bill), in addition to dozens of politicians, government officials, and business leaders.

The basic design of the opportunity zone legislation is to incentivize investors to (i) realize capital gains in the broader market in exchange for near-term and long-term tax benefits, and (ii) reinvest the gains in real estate development and operating business activities in low-income communities.   According to EIG, United States households held unrealized capital gains of $3.8 trillion and domestic corporations held an additional $2.2 trillion of unrealized capital gains.[4] EIG provided significant support for the proposition that investment in low-income communities and distressed communities are not receiving an adequate share of investment activities in the United States.[5]

In general, the opportunity zone legislation turned out to be much broader in application as compared to previous tax incentive programs designed to spur investment in low-income communities.  The larger scope of the program is possible due to a number of factors including, among others:

**Geographic Scope of QOZ Program.**  The geographic scope of the opportunity zone program is huge.  Under the first part of the legislation, 25-percent of the low-income census tracts in the United States were nominated as "qualified opportunity zones" by the respective Governors of every state (in addition to the District of Columbia and US Possessions). According to the Congressional Research Service, there were 8,761 census tracts (equal to 25-percent of the total eligible census tracts, adjusted for the 25-percent census tract minimum per State) nominated as qualified opportunity zones.[6]  With approximately 74,000 census tracts, this equates to approximately 12 percent of the entire country.

**No Dollar Limitations**. The benefits under the program are not limited to a fixed, annual dollar amount requiring allocation by government officials. Also, the complexity of the opportunity zone program is reduced for investors, developers and municipalities, as compared to prior programs such as the New Market Tax Credit or Enterprise Zones Tax Credit, both of which require investors to understand how to obtain and use qualifying tax credits to offset current year income.

**(Relatively) Easy to Understand**. The tax incentives are relatively easy to understand for investors, developers and business owners with substantial tax benefits realized immediately (through capital gains deferral), while the most significant tax benefit (tax-free appreciation) is achieved only after the expected benefits to low-income communities are realized. Thus, the coordination of the benefits for investors and developers, and the realization of the desired outcomes for communities are aligned to achieve short- and long-term goals.

**Large Number of Potential Participants**. Given the sheer volume of individuals and businesses that incur capital gains on a regular basis, the number of stakeholders that may benefit from investing under the program is vast. Moreover, since capital gains are constantly being generated, the ability to benefit will recur time and again during the life of the program.

## SUMMARY OF QUALIFIED OPPORTUNITY ZONES

The qualified opportunity zone legislation was passed into law under the TCJA, effective for tax years after December 31, 2017. The genesis of the law is that Republicans and Democrats, with a focus on improving low-income communities, backed legislation that would incentivize taxpayers to unlock capital gains and reinvest those gains into these communities. There were two parts to the QOZ legislation passed under the TCJA.

The first part of the legislation authorized each State (in addition to the District of Columbia and US possessions) to designate twenty-five percent of the low-income census tracts in such State as "qualified opportunity zones". The designation process was completed and the zones were finalized in June 2018.[7]

The second part of the legislation provided tax incentives to investors. Specifically, the law provides the following tax benefits to investors that reinvest capital gains into a qualified opportunity fund ("QOF"):

**Deferral of Capital Gains.** A taxpayer that reinvests capital gains within the 180-day period beginning on the date such gain was recognized, in a QOF, may defer the gain until the earlier of (i) the date that the taxpayer sells or exchanges its QOF investment; or (ii) December 31, 2026.[8]

**Step-Up in Basis (Elimination of a Portion of Original Deferred Gain)**. If the taxpayer holds its investment in the QOF for at least 5 years, 10-percent of the original gain will be eliminated. If the taxpayer holds its investment in the QOF for at least 7 years, an additional 5-percent of the original gain will be eliminated (for a total of 15-percent). To obtain the 7-year benefit, an investment must have been made by December 31, 2019, and to meet the 5-year test an investment must have been made by December 31, 2021.

**Tax-Free Appreciation**. If the taxpayer holds its investment in the QOF for ten years, all of the capital gain attributable to the appreciation in the QOF (in excess of the original investment which will be taxed in 2026) will be tax-free when the taxpayer disposes of its interests in the QOF.

**Avoid Recapture.**   Typically, a leveraged real estate or private equity investment generates tax losses for many years due to depreciation and amortization of assets acquired with debt. When such investment is sold, these losses are "recaptured" (*i.e.*, create additional taxable income when the losses are reversed). A QOF will generate the same tax losses, however, many taxpayers would avoid "recapture", resulting in the taxpayer benefiting from deductions over time that may <u>never</u> be offset with additional income.

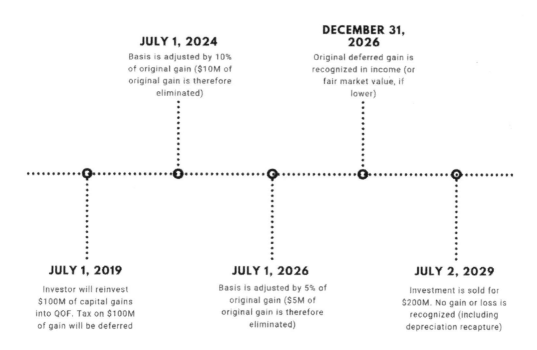

**JULY 1, 2024**
Basis is adjusted by 10% of original gain ($10M of original gain is therefore eliminated)

**DECEMBER 31, 2026**
Original deferred gain is recognized in income (or fair market value, if lower)

**JULY 1, 2019**
Investor will reinvest $100M of capital gains into QOF. Tax on $100M of gain will be deferred

**JULY 1, 2026**
Basis is adjusted by 5% of original gain ($5M of original gain is therefore eliminated)

**JULY 2, 2029**
Investment is sold for $200M. No gain or loss is recognized (including depreciation recapture)

Note that prior to the completion of the ten-year holding period, the taxpayer will pay (in 2027) the tax on the lesser of the (A) remaining deferred capital gains for the 2026 tax year reduced by any QOF basis adjustments; or (B) the fair market value of its equity investment (determined as of December 31, 2026 under the QOZ regulations), reduced by any QOF basis adjustments as applicable. The QOF basis adjustment will either be 0-percent, 10-percent or 15-percent of the original deferred gain, depending on the taxpayer's holding period.

**Thus, the taxpayer will defer and reduce (but not eliminate) the tax on the original invested capital. If the taxpayer meets the statutory requirements, the tax on the gain relating to the appreciation of the investment may be completely eliminated *regardless of the amount of such gain*. Accordingly, there is no limit to the amount of gains that may be eliminated under the QOZ legislation.**

**Ultimately, the effect of these tax benefits is to greatly enhance an investor's return (as compared to a traditional investment without such tax benefits). Most fund-type investments will reflect an increased return of 25-percent to 50-percent.**

The qualified opportunity fund program created an entirely new set of terminology (a literal alphabet soup of new terms).

The following listing of abbreviations may be necessary to capture the essence of the program structure (the full listing of key terms is described in *Appendix A: The ABCs of OZs*):

| ABBREVIATION | MEANING |
|---|---|
| QOF | Qualified Opportunity Fund (an investment vehicle to invest in QOZP) |
| QOZ | Qualified Opportunity Zone means the census tracts designated as qualified opportunity zones. |
| QOZP | Qualified Opportunity Zone Property means either a "qualified opportunity zone partnership interest", "qualified opportunity zone stock" or QOZBP. |
| QOZBP | Qualified Opportunity Zone Business Property means property that meets certain acquisition, use or improvement and physical location attributes. |
| QOZB | To qualify as "qualified opportunity zone partnership interest" or "qualified opportunity zone stock", such business must meet the definition of a QOZB. A QOZB is a business that meets various criteria, including holding at least 70-percent of its interest as QOZBP. |

In order to achieve the tax benefits offered by the opportunity zone legislation noted above, the investor must reinvest capital gains in a QOF. A QOZ investment will either be structured as a (A) QOF that directly owns QOZBP, or (B) by a QOF that operates a QOZB partnership or corporation.

In each case, three requirements must be met to be considered qualified property:

**Acquisition Requirement**. The property must be acquired by purchase or lease after December 31, 2017;

**Original Use or Substantial Improvement Test**. The original use of the property must commence with the QOF or the property must be substantially improved by the QOF; and

**Substantially All Test for Holding Period and Use of Property**. During at least 90-percent of the holding period of such property, at least 70-percent of the use of the property must be used in the QOZ.

The use of a partnership or corporation that is operated as a qualified opportunity zone business is preferable in most cases. Using this structure, a QOF will meet the 90-percent test so long as the underlying partnership or corporation is itself a QOZB.[9]

The primary reason that the use of a QOZB is beneficial is that a QOZB may avail itself of a 31-month working capital safe harbor (treating cash, cash equivalents and short-term loans as "good" property during the 31-month period). Also, only 70-percent of the tangible property of a QOZB must be qualified property (instead of 90-percent). These benefits typically outweigh any disadvantages (see below chart) of the QOZB structure.

On the other hand, a QOF that owns QOZBP directly (rather than conducting a QOZB through a partnership or corporation) is required to have 90-percent of its property be qualified property. Moreover, only cash contributed during the prior 6 months is considered "good" property if held as cash, cash equivalents or short-term loans. After that time period, any financial property (*e.g.*, cash, securities) is considered nonqualified, which would cause the QOF to potentially fail the 90-percent asset holding test.

The chart below illustrates the difference between these two approaches:

| QOF THAT OWNS QOZBP DIRECTLY | QOF THAT OWNS QOZB PARTNERSHIP INTERESTS |
| --- | --- |
| 90-percent of QOF's assets must be QOZBP | 70-percent of QOZB's assets must be QOZBP |
| Working capital safe harbor does not apply. Intangible and financial assets (e.g., cash) will be treated as nonqualifying assets for purposes of 90-percent test | The working capital safe harbor allows for cash, cash equivalents and short-term debt obligations held for use subject to a written plan to be ignored for purposes of calculating the 70-percent test for up to 31 months |
| No active conduct standard | 50-percent gross income from active trade or business requirement |
| Intangible property counts towards the 90-percent test (as a nonqualifying asset) | Can own an unlimited amount of intangible property so long as 40-percent is used in the active conduct of a trade or business. |
| No restrictions on type of businesses | Prohibition on "sin" businesses |

**Therefore, most projects and businesses will be structured using a two-tier structure such that a QOF (or multiple QOFs) own interests in a partnership that is qualified as a QOZB.**

The following represents a sample structure reflecting the use of a QOZB:

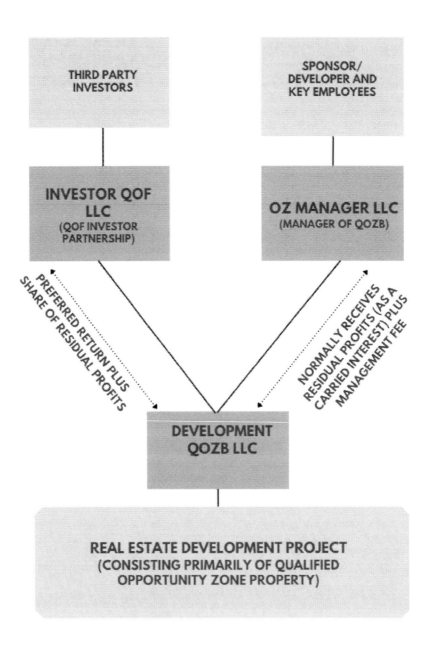

*The following detailed example reflects the timeline of a QOF:*

1.  Investors makes investment on July 1, 2019 of $10,000,000 (of reinvested gains that would have been recognized during the prior 180 days) in QOF. Investors will defer capital gains on such $10,000,000.

2.  QOF contributes $10,000,000 of cash on July 1, 2019 to QOZP Sub (which is a qualified opportunity zone partnership interest). Since QOZP Sub is a partnership for tax purposes, it must have a second partner. This may be a sponsor or employee, or may be another QOF (related or unrelated).

3.  QOZP Sub acquires land and building on July 2, 2019 for $10,000,000 of cash, and then enters into construction loan for $20,000,000. QOZ Sub begins to make improvements to the Property using funds under the construction loan.

4.  From July 2, 2019 through December 31, 2021, the QOZP Sub constructs improvements on the Property greater than the allocated cost of the acquired tangible property. This will satisfy the substantial improvement test. During this time, the working capital safe harbor will apply (with a 31-month period applying to all cash received as contributions or loans, beginning on the date of receipt).

5.  On March 15, 2020 (or September 15, 2020 if extended), the QOF files its initial partnership tax return (Form 1065). The partnership will self-certify as a QOF by filing Form 8996 with its 2019 tax return and select July 2019 as the initial month of the QOF.

Likewise, QOZP Sub will file its partnership tax return (but will not be required to file Form 8996).

6. On April 15, 2020 (or October 15, 2020 if extended), the Investors will file their individual tax returns. On their individual returns, the Investors will defer capital gains by making the appropriate election on Form 8949. Each investor will also file Form 8997 reporting all of its QOF related investments.

7. On July 1, 2024, the Investors will receive a basis adjustment equal to $1,000,000 with respect to their investment. The effect of this adjustment is to eliminate $1,000,000 of the initial capital gains (*i.e.*, the 10-percent reduction on $10,000,000 investment after 5 years).

8. On July 1, 2026, the Investors will receive a basis adjustment equal to $500,000 with respect to their investment. The effect of this adjustment is to eliminate $500,000 of the initial capital gains (*i.e.*, the additional 5-percent reduction on $10,000,000 investment after 5 years).

9. On December 31, 2026, the Investors will recognize the lesser of (1) $8,500,000 of capital gains (equal to the deferred capital gains, less the 15-percent basis adjustment) or (2) the fair market value of their investment, less the 15-percent basis adjustment. Assuming that the investment has not declined in value, the investors will have tax liability of approximately $2,720,000 (assuming a 32-percent tax rate). Following the inclusion of capital gain, the Investor will have basis in its investment (excluding debt basis) of $10,000,000.

10. On April 15, 2027, the Investors will pay the tax liability of $2,720,000 with their timely filed tax return or extension (subject to estimated tax liabilities that would cause payment to be made during 2026).

11. On July 3, 2029, the Investors sell their investment in the QOF for $25,000,000. Alternatively, the QOZP Sub may sell the Property (and pay off liabilities) with net distributable proceeds of $25,000,000. At this time, the Investors have basis in their investment of $0 (after additional depreciation deductions have reduced basis from the $8,500,000 included in 2026 to $0).

12. On April 15, 2030, The Investors will make an election to adjust the basis of their investment to fair market value at the time of sale.[10] The Investors will recognize no gain on the sale of their interests. Since the Investors had basis of $0, the $25,000,000 of gain that is excluded from income results in tax savings of approximately $8,750,000 (assuming a blended 35-percent tax rate, including unrecaptured §1250 gain).

CHAPTER TWO

# Investor Roadmap and Planning Concepts

The qualified opportunity zone ("QOZ") program is based on the premise that investors will reinvest their profits from their investment activities (including sales of closely held stock or real estate) in a qualified opportunity fund ("QOF") for a minimum ten-year holding period. A QOF is, basically, an investment vehicle that will invest in real estate development projects or operating businesses located in a "qualified opportunity zone" (generally consisting of low-income communities throughout the country). To the extent that an investor reinvests capital gain into a QOF, such investor will be eligible for substantial tax benefits that have the effect of increasing its after-tax return on the investment. In many cases, an investor's internal rate of return ("IRR") will be increased by nearly 50-percent or more in many cases because of the tax benefits under the program.

The tax benefits available to an investor consist of the (1) deferral of invested capital gains until December 31, 2026; (2) reduction of the original capital gain of up to 15-percent (or more, in certain circumstances); and (3) tax-free appreciation if the investment is held at least ten years (including no recognition of depreciation recapture) if structured properly.

## LIFE CYCLE OF AN INVESTMENT IN A QOF (INVESTOR'S PERSPECTIVE)

The life cycle of an investor in a QOF can be summarized in the following scenario. Note that the below scenario reflects an example of one particular investment structure and a selected method of eventual disposition. Different choices are available depending on the facts (and desired outcomes) of a particular investment and related transactions.

Assume that the proposed investment requires that investors (collectively) invest $100 million into a QOF in exchange for a membership interest that provides for an 8% preferred return on unreturned invested capital (compounded annually) and 60% of all residual profits after payment of the preferred return.[11] The remaining 40% of the residual profits (after payment of the preferred return) is the sponsor's promote interest. Assume that the QOF (or underlying operating entities) borrows $200 million (pursuant to a construction loan) to fund development expenses for a single real estate development project, resulting in total cost of the project of $300 million.[12] The investment will close (*i.e.*, the funds will be contributed) on April 30, 2019. We further assume that the property will be sold on May 1, 2029 for $600 million (reflecting a compounded annual growth rate of approximately 7.2%).

## Step 1: Pre-Investment Activities (January 1, 2018 - April 30, 2019)

The Investor must recognize capital gain of $100M during the 180-day period preceding the date of the investment. The recognized capital gain may either (i) consist of capital gains that were recognized upon the sale or exchange of a capital asset during the 180-day period preceding the investment (November 1, 2018 through April 30, 2019 in our example); or (ii) capital gains that are considered to be recognized on the last day of the 2018 tax year (§1231 gains, §1256 gains, or certain distributions of capital gains by REITs or RICs).

Capital gains that are recognized by a pass-through entity (partnership, S corporation, trust or estate) may be recognized by the partner under the regular 180-day rule, the last day of the tax year (*i.e.*, December 31) or the unextended due date of the entity tax return (*i.e.*, March 15 for partnerships and S corporations). Thus, a partner in a partnership may choose to use either (1) the actual date of the sale or exchange, (2) the last day of the tax year, or (3) the unextended due date of the partnership tax return, to start the clock for the 180-day period.

An investor in a QOF may be an individual or entity. An investor may not reinvest gains recognized from a sale to a related party.

## Step 2: Making the Investment (April 30, 2019)

The investor that incurred the capital gain should directly invest in a QOF (the use of a single member LLC is permitted but a contribution of cash or property to another partnership or S corporation that in turn invests in a QOF is not explicitly permitted). The investment must be considered equity for tax purposes. Thus, a convertible debt instrument or similar structure will not qualify as an investment under the QOZ program.

The investment may be in the form of either cash or property. However, if an investor contributes property, the amount of the qualifying investment (eligible for QOZ tax benefits) is equal to the adjusted basis of the contributed property; the fair market value of property in excess of such amount will be a non-qualifying investment which is not eligible for any of the QOZ tax benefits (it will be treated like a normal real estate investment). Similarly, if an investor contributes cash for an equity investment that exceeds the investor's capital gains during the applicable 180-day period, the portion in excess of recognized capital gains will be a non-qualifying investment.

A QOF may be either a partnership or corporation. There is no requirement that a QOF be "fund" in the traditional usage of the term (*i.e.*, comparable to a private equity fund or similar structure). Rather, a QOF may be a closely held partnership with two or more partners or be structured as a fund with many investors. A QOF corporation may have a single owner.

## Step 3: Making the Election (April 15, 2020 or the extended due date)

The investor must make an election by reporting the exclusion from income on Form 8949 of its tax return by specifying which gains will be deferred. A pass-through entity may make the election to defer gain. However, if such pass-through entity does not make the election, the individual (which may be a partner, shareholder or beneficiary) may make the election on their respective income tax filing (such as a Form 1040). In addition, the Investor must file Form 8997 reporting all of its QOF investments.

## Step 4: Construction Phase and Commencement of Rental Activity (April 30, 2019 - April 30, 2024)

During the initial five years of the project, the project will be constructed using the invested proceeds and the construction loan. During this timeframe, the project will be nearly identical from an economic and tax perspective as compared to a traditional real estate investment. The one major tax difference is that the investor will have no basis in its qualified investment (but it will have debt basis for operating distributions and losses, but not for debt financed distributions within 2 years). Thus, for partnership investors, the tax treatment will in most cases be the same as a regular investment (so long as the investors are allocated their proportionate share of qualified nonrecourse liabilities). Investors in an S corporation will not be so lucky, as the lack of stock basis will cause all losses to be at-risk and suspended.

Following the completion of construction and the commencement of rental activities (until the property is stabilized), the project would likely be refinanced with a permanent loan. To the extent that such refinancing allows for debt financed distributions to the preferred investors, the investors will be able to use debt basis after 2 years to avoid tax (or the inclusion of previously deferred gains).

During the early years of the project, it is likely that the project will generate tax losses (due in large part to the allowable depreciation of the $300M costs and the higher amount of interest expense in the early years of a loan). Losses are likely even if the project generates distributable cash flow. In other words, the project will have essentially the same tax attributes as a traditional leveraged real estate investment.

## Step 5: Basis Adjustment on April 30, 2024 (Will Not Apply for Investments Made after December 31, 2019)

On April 30, 2024, the Investor will have held its investment for five (5) years. Accordingly, the Investor's basis in their interest in the QOF will be increased by 10-percent of the original deferred gain (an increase of $10 million). Thus, in our example, the investor (that originally invested cash of $100 million) will have basis of $10 million following this basis adjustment.

## Step 6: Basis Adjustment on April 30, 2026 (Will Not Apply for Investments Made after December 31, 2021)

On April 30, 2024, the Investor will have held its investment for seven (7) years. Accordingly, the Investor's basis in their interest in the QOF will be increased by an additional 5-percent of the original deferred gain (for a total of 15-percent) (an increase of $5 million). Thus, in our example, the investor (that originally invested cash of $100 million) will have basis of $15 million following this second basis adjustment.

## Step 7: Inclusion of Gain on December 31, 2026

On December 31, 2026, the Investor must recognize in income the amount of the remaining deferred gain (or the fair market value of the investment, if less than the remaining deferred gain), less the amount of the basis adjustments for meeting the five- and seven-year holding periods (described in Steps 5 and 6). The tax attribute of the gains included in income will be the same as if the gains had been included in 2019 (*i.e.*, short or long term, collectibles, §1231, or 1256 gains). The tax rate, however, will be the tax rates applicable in the year of inclusion.

Assuming that the fair market value of the investment did not decrease, the investor will recognize $85 million of gain (which will increase its basis by $85 million).

If the QOF is a partnership (which is normally the case), the general fair market value rule will not be applicable. Instead, the partner will recognize gain equal to the lesser of (1) the remaining deferred gain, less the 5-year and 7-year basis adjustments as applicable, or (2) the taxable gain that would result if the investment was sold in a fully taxable transaction at fair market value (which is assumed to be greater than $100M in this example).

## Step 8: Continued Operations Until May 1, 2029

From 2026 through 2029, the project will continue operations. It is anticipated that by this point in the lifetime of the project, the annual distributions will at least cover the preferred return. Ideally, the project will maximize value upon the sale or exchange following a ten-year holding period. In generally economic terms, it is possible that the expiration of the ten-year holding period (over the 3-5 year period in which most QOFs were funded) will create glut of sellers. In some markets, this could cause relative oversupply (which could decrease prices). An investor may weigh the market conditions against the after-tax return of continuing to own the investment.

Note that an investor will have until 2047 to sell its investment and be eligible for the tax benefits. A longer holding period can reduce the risk that excess supply of QOZ properties will negatively impact prices and investor returns.

## Step 9: Disposition of the Property (May 1, 2029)

On May 1, 2029, the property (which cost $300 million to construct) will be sold for $600 million. After repayment of debt (approximately $147 million) and payment of transaction costs (approximately $20 million), the balance of $433 million will be distributed to the partners in accordance with the respective operating agreements of the QOF and its subsidiary entities. To the extent that the refinance at the time of permanent financing and cash flow from operations covered the payment for preferred return (but not the principal), the distribution to partners at the time of the sale will be approximately (i) $100 million return of invested capital to preferred investors; (ii) $200 million to preferred members (equal to 60% of residual cash flow) and (iii) $133 million with respect to the promote interest (equal to 40% of residual cash flow). Thus, the project generated a pre-tax return for the investors of 16.61% (calculated using the Excel XIRR formula).

To the extent that the property (consisting of personal property, qualified improvements, residential rental property and commercial rental property) was depreciated from $300 million to $100 million, the investors have capital account balances of negative $100 million. Thus, the sale of the property (under normal tax rules) for $600 million would generate taxable gain of $680 million (after taking into account transaction costs of $20 million). Of this amount, $200 million consists of depreciation recapture (assumed to be §1250 gain taxed an aggregate federal and state tax rate of 37-percent) and the remainder is capital gain (taxed at an aggregate federal and state tax rate of 32-percent). Accordingly, the estimated federal and state tax liability resulting from the sale if no election is made (as described in Step 10 below) will be $228 million.

## Step 10: Making the Election with respect to the Sale of the Investment or Property (April 15, 2030)

The taxpayer may avoid the taxable gain (including the $200 million (described in §9 above) recapture income that is treated as capital gains) resulting from the disposition of the property by making an election to exclude the capital gain arising from the disposition as reported on the investor's K-1 received from the QOF. Note that there is also an election to step up the basis in the investment at the time the investment is sold or exchanged (which would not be the structure that is generally utilized in a sale of real estate assets). In either case, the investor will not have taxable capital gains with respect to the disposition of the property.

# APPLICABILITY OF OPPORTUNITY ZONE PROGRAM FOR INVESTORS

In order for an investor (the "Investor") to maximize tax benefits under the QOZ program, the investor will need to take the following steps:

1. Recognize capital gains.
2. Select a Qualified Opportunity Fund (or form a new QOF)
3. Invest in a QOF (within the applicable time period).
4. Elect to defer capital gains.
5. (Potentially) increase the basis of the investment in the QOF.
6. Recognize all or a portion of the previously deferred capital gains in income.
7. Elect to step up basis upon disposition to eliminate tax liability.

## THE INVESTOR MUST RECOGNIZE CAPITAL GAINS.

The threshold requirement is that an investor in a QOF ("Investor") must recognize capital gains. The timing of gain recognition is critical. To obtain the tax incentives, an amount of money equal to the amount of capital gains that the taxpayer desires to defer must be invested in a qualified opportunity fund within 180 days of the date that the capital gain is recognized for income tax purposes.

For purposes of the QOZ program, a capital gain means any gain that is treated as capital gains for federal income tax purposes that would be recognized prior to January 1, 2027 (and does not arise from a sale or exchange with a related party). The gains may be short term or long term, §1231 gains, §1250 gains, §1256 gains or collectibles gains (or any other gains that are used to calculate federal capital gains tax).

Note that unlike the most widely recognized tax-deferral strategy, a like-kind exchange governed by §1031, the QOF program does not require careful tracing of cash. Rather, the only requirement is that the cash or property is invested, and that the investor had that amount of recognized capital gains that it elects to defer.

The following chart reflects when gain is recognized for federal income tax purposes (such that the 180-day period commences for meeting the reinvested gains requirement):

| TYPE OF GAINS | TIMING OF GAIN RECOGNITION |
|---|---|
| Regular Capital Gains | Gain recognized at the time of the sale or exchange (on the trade date, in the case of marketable securities) |
| REIT and RIC Capital Gains | Date that the dividend is paid |
| REIT and RIC Undistributed Capital Gains | Last day of the tax year of the REIT or RIC |
| §1231 Gains | Gain recognized on last day of the investor's tax year equal to the *gross* §1231 gain for the year |
| §1256 Gains | Gain recognized on last day of tax year equal to the investor's net §1256 gain for the year (offsetting-position transactions are not eligible) |
| Gain Resulting from a Shift in §752 Liabilities | Not eligible to defer gains with deemed 752 gains |
| Special Rule for Pass Through Entities | In the case of partnerships, S corporations, estate and trusts, the taxpayer will treat the gain as occurring on the last day of the investor's tax year or the unextended due date of the partnership's tax return, unless the taxpayer elects to treat the date as occurring on the date that gain is otherwise recognized by the pass through entity for federal income tax purposes |

## THE INVESTOR MUST SELECT A QOF OR FORM A NEW QOF.

The investor must choose to invest in a third party QOF (many of which are being formed and operated as real estate or private equity funds) or to form its own QOF with respect to a closely held business or real estate investment. The program does not permit a QOF to invest in another QOF.

Third-party funds with professional managers are being formed regularly to invest in projects or companies that enable such fund to qualify as a QOF. Effectively, the investment opportunities are comparable to funds in the marketplace today (except, of course, that a QOF must invest in property in a QOZ and follow the myriad of rules set forth in the QOZ program) including leveraged real estate QOFs and venture capital QOFs.

Since a QOF may be any partnership or corporation that properly invests in qualified property, a closely held QOF is easy to form and not overly costly to maintain. All QOFs must meet the various criteria discussed below in terms of QOF compliance and structure.

### THE INVESTOR MUST INVEST IN A QOF (WITHIN 180 DAYS OF RECOGNIZING GAINS)

During the 180-day period beginning on the date that capital gains are recognized (see above chart), the investor must invest an amount of cash (or the adjusted basis of property) into a QOF. The investment must be treated as an equity investment for income tax purposes. Thus, an investment structured as convertible debt will not qualify as an eligible investment (although the conversion to equity should be able to qualify as an eligible investment at the time of conversion).

*Potential Pitfalls for Investors*

Investors must be very careful if they intend to contribute property to a QOF. If the contributed property has a fair market value in excess of the adjusted basis of such property, the value in excess of the adjusted basis will be considered a nonqualified investment that is not eligible for the tax benefits under the QOZ program (the amount attributable to the property's adjusted basis will be a qualified investment).  As noted above, the amount of gain deferred for contributions of property will be the adjusted basis of the property (and not fair market value).

An investor is permitted to acquire a QOF interest from an existing QOF owner (*i.e.*, a sale in the secondary market).  The purchased interest will be treated as qualifying property (and gains up the amount of the purchase price can be deferred from income).  Note that an investor's holding period begins as of the date of purchase.  Thus, if an interest is acquired in the secondary market (such that an investor's holding period begins as of the date that the investment was acquired in the secondary market) and the property will be sold by the QOF prior to the ten-year period, the secondary market purchaser will not be able to avail itself of the tax-free appreciation rule.

 The issuance of a profits interest in exchange for services will not be considered a qualified investment.  Thus, the owner of a carried interest will not be eligible for the tax benefits under the QOZ program.  Investors that contribute cash and also receive a profits interest should carefully structure their interests to avoid having a disproportionate share of their interests taxed under regular tax rules.

## THE INVESTOR MUST ELECT TO DEFER CAPITAL GAINS

The investor must defer capital gains.  A taxpayer that may make such deferral election includes an individual, partnership, S corporation, C corporation, trust, or estate.  If gains are incurred by an entity, the deferral may be made by the entity that previously incurred capital gains eligible for reinvestment.  If the entity (or any upper-tier entity that is a direct or indirect owner of such entity) does not make the election to defer gains, the individual partners may elect to defer gains on their individual tax return.

The investor (whether an individual or an entity) will make the election by identifying the gains that will be deferred in accordance with IRS instructions on Form 8949 and Schedule D of the applicable tax return. A taxpayer may use any portion of a larger gain for multiple investments. The taxpayer will also file Form 8997 to report all of its QOF investments.

### THE INVESTOR MAY ADJUST THE BASIS OF ITS INVESTMENT

The Investor is entitled to tax benefits (accomplished through increases to the basis of the Investor's investment) by meeting certain holding period requirements. After the Investor has held its investment in a QOF for at least 5 years it will increase its basis in the investment by10-percent of the original deferred gain. After the investor has held its investment in a QOF for at least 7 years it will increase its basis in the investment by an additional 5-percent of the original deferred gain. These basis adjustments have the effect of eliminating the tax liability of up to 15-percent percent of the original deferred gain.

### THE INVESTOR WILL RECOGNIZE PREVIOUSLY DEFERRED GAIN.

The investor will recognize a portion of the previously deferred gain on the earlier of (A) the date that the investment (or any portion) is sold or exchanged (or deemed to be sold or exchanged due to an inclusion event) or (B) December 31, 2026. In some cases, an investment will be treated as disposed of, for purposes of including previously deferred gains (in whole or in part), if it is sold, transferred, gifted, contributed, or liquidated (any such event is considered an "inclusion event"). Likewise, if the QOF engages in a transaction that results in an investor recognizing gain (*i.e.*, with respect to distributions in excess of basis, or taxable boot in a non-recognition transaction), the investor will be considered to have sold or exchanged a portion of its investment. The transfer of equity ownership of upper-tier entities may also result in previously deferred gain being included in income.

In most cases, if a QOF or an investor engages in a transfer that is treated as a non-recognition transaction (under partnership or corporate rules), previously deferred gain will not be included in income. Similarly, a transfer by an investor to a grantor trust (which is treated as owned by the grantor for income tax purposes) will not result in gain inclusion. The receipt by an estate (or distribution from an estate) of a QOF interest is not an inclusion event.

On December 31, 2026, the Investor will recognize an amount in income equal to the lesser of (A) the remaining deferred gain or (B) the fair market value of the investment as of that date, less the amount of basis adjustments (due to the statutory adjustments based on the investor's holding period or with respect to a prior gain inclusion).[13] A modified rule applies to partnerships that measures the gain included by reference to the gain that would result in a taxable sale of the investment as of December 31, 2026.

The effect of the "lesser of" rule is that a taxpayer will need to ascertain the fair market value of its investment as of the date of any inclusion event (including December 31, 2026) and compare this amount with its deferred capital gain. If the value of the investment is less, the Investor will only recognize an amount of income equal to such fair market value (less allowable basis). The fair market value should be determined under normal federal income tax principles (including the applicability of discounts for lack of control and lack of marketability).

### THE INVESTOR WILL AVOID GAIN UPON THE DISPOSITION OF QUALIFIED PROPERTY.

After the Investor has held its investment for 10 years, the sale or exchange of such investment will be tax free. The Investor accomplishes tax free treatment by making an election to (A) increase its basis in its investment to the fair market value or (B) exclude the capital gain arising from the disposition of qualified property by the QOF.

Since the tax-free appreciation is adjusted through a step-up in basis to fair market value, the Investor (in a properly structured transaction) will never have any depreciation recapture with respect to a qualified investment for which such election is made. This will not prevent the Investor from recognizing losses (whether active or passive) during the time period in which the investment is held.

# ECONOMIC OUTCOMES FOR QUALIFIED OPPORTUNITY ZONE INVESTORS

Investors typically use the internal rate of return (IRR) concept as a metric to measure the return on an investment in the context of a leveraged real estate investment. The IRR model reflects the compounded annual return of a series of cash flows. In the context of an opportunity zone investment, we can measure the effect of the tax benefits under the program by treating such tax benefits or liabilities as cash paid or received at the time the tax would otherwise have been paid without regard to the opportunity zone program.

We can compute the (1) tax liability that is *not* paid on the date of the investment (or the date that such tax liability would have been due), (2) tax that will be paid on an inclusion date or December 31, 2026 (since the tax would normally be due on April 15, 2027) and (3) tax that is not paid at the time of sale. These three tax amounts can then be treated as additional cash inflows or outflows (since they would normally be paid/received by an investor that is basing return on a pre-tax IRR) which can be entered into the IRR formula to determine the pre-tax IRR. This approach is described below as the "IRR" approach.

Arguably, this method overstates the IRR since it assumes the tax liability on the deferred capital gain is invested at the full project level IRR (as if the saved taxes are invested in the transaction). It may not be accurate to suggest that an Investor increased its investment to account for the immediate tax savings. Thus, an alternative method to measure the deferred capital gain savings is using a basic present value formula at conservative interest rate (which makes sense for investors that would invest the money to pay this future tax liability using a lower risk asset allocation). This approach is described below as the "NPV" approach.

We have therefore modeled our IRR comparisons using each of the respective approaches. We have used a projection prepared for a development project that generated a pre-tax IRR of 14.72% with a disposition of the property after 10 years. The IRR of a QOF that obtained all of the tax benefits (whether using NPV or reinvestment of tax savings) is significantly higher as set forth in the table below:

|     | Normal IRR | IRR with QOZ Benefits | *Increase* |
| --- | --- | --- | --- |
| **NPV** | **14.72%** | **19.57%** | *32.91%* |
| **IRR** | **14.72%** | **21.53%** | *46.19%* |

This example is consistent with prior deals that we have analyzed which reflect an increase in the return of 25-50-percent. There is no predictable way to model general corporate investment, however, similar benefits would apply to the average return for private equity or venture fund investments.[14]

# CHAPTER THREE

# Maximizing Value for Real Estate Developers

The industry that most obviously should benefit from the opportunity zone program is the real estate development business.

First, the tax incentives for real estate investors in the opportunity zone program are relatively predictable. For example, if real estate is held for ten years, there is a decreased risk (as compared to an operating business) that timing of the property disposition will have a drastic effect on investors' return (valuations of stabilized real estate assets are less volatile over an extended time horizon). Most leveraged real estate investments generate substantial depreciation deductions and the opportunity zone program allows for the depreciation recapture to be eliminated. This allows leveraged real estate investments that do not meet expectations to nonetheless have acceptable after-tax returns for a QOZ investment.

Second, a real estate investment is relatively easy to qualify for the QOZ program. Since the mechanical rules provide for strict guidelines on timing of the capital investment, location of physical property and performance of services, a real estate QOF has less risk of failing conform to QOF guidelines. Unlike an operating business that may require capital as the business needs dictate, additional capital is less likely to be required after the initial construction phase of a real estate project (which makes it easier for all investors to obtain tax benefits under the QOZ program). The fact that real estate will be physically located in the QOZ eliminates the risk that the QOF will cease to qualify as business operations cause activities to be conducted (in a substantial manner) out of the QOZ.

## LIFE CYCLE OF A LEVERAGED REAL ESTATE QOF (FROM THE PERSPECTIVE OF A REAL ESTATE DEVELOPER OR SPONSOR)

The following steps reflect the life cycle of a leveraged real estate QOF and the steps and decisions that the developer or sponsor must take in connection with the formation, operations and ultimate disposition of the project.

We assume the same fact pattern as in the previous example (in Part 2), as follows:

Assume that the proposed investment requires that investors (collectively) invest $100 million into a QOF in exchange for a membership interest that provides for an 8% preferred return on unreturned invested capital (compounded annually) and 60% of all residual profits after payment of the preferred return. The remaining 40% of the residual profits (after payment of the preferred return) is the sponsor's promote interest. Assume that the QOF (or underlying operating entities) borrows $200 million (pursuant to a construction loan) to fund development expenses for a single real estate development project (the "Project"), resulting in total cost of the project of $300 million. The investment will close (*i.e.*, the funds will be contributed) on April 30, 2019. We further assume that the property will be sold on May 1, 2029 for $600 million (reflecting a compounded annual growth rate of approximately 7.2%).

## Step 1: Pre-Development Activities (January 1, 2018 - April 30, 2019)

Frequently, a real estate developer will begin pre-development activities prior to the actual acquisition of real property. In some cases, a developer will have a property under contract based on contingencies to obtain governmental approvals, zoning changes, and permits. These activities include preliminary due diligence, certain aspects of the entitlement process, engaging in negotiations with potential tenants and other soft costs.

In the context of a QOF investing in real estate, such pre-development assets (*i.e.*, the soft costs incurred for pre-development activities) will not be considered QOZP. Accordingly, the developer will need to determine whether such assets should be contributed or sold to the QOF when it is formed. Likewise, if a developer intended to use capital gains to fund its investment, it may make sense to fund pre-development costs through a loan to the operating entity, which will be repaid (with interest) following the date that the entity elects to be treated as a QOF.

## Step 2: Capital Raising Activities (January 1, 2018 - April 30, 2019)

Once the project is "ready to go", the developer or sponsor must line up capital. However, in this context, the developer or sponsor must cause the investors to contribute capital up to the amount of capital gains recognized (and deferred) by such investor during the applicable 180-day timeframe (if such investors intend to benefit from opportunity zones). Thus, the typical structure of a leveraged real estate fund (with many projects owned directly by the fund) is generally not recommended for a QOF. Instead, the QOFs will either be set up separately for each project or the capital could be called all at once and will then be held by the QOF until it is needed.

## Step 3: Structuring the QOF (April 2019)

The developer/sponsor should structure its project in order to maximize the tax benefits under the QOZ program. To accomplish this result, the developer will form three limited liability companies that will be treated as partnerships for tax purposes (this structure is used so that the QOF may benefit from the specific benefits available for a QOZB). The following chart reflects the general investment structure.

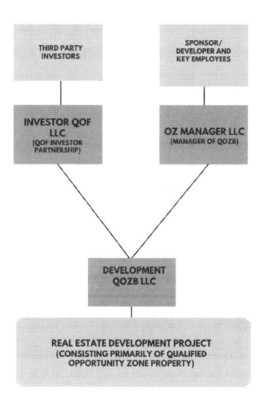

Investor QOF LLC ("InvestCo") and OZ Manager LLC ("ManagerCo") are the owners of Development QOZB LLC ("OpCo"). InvestCo will be treated as a QOF. ManagerCo will normally not be treated as a QOF since it receives a carried interest and QOF treatment would be inefficient (contributions by the developer should be made through a separate QOF).

The organizational documents for InvestCo will include a provision providing that the QOF was formed for the purpose of investing in QOZP.

OpCo is treated as a QOZ partnership interest. Accordingly, the operating business may (i) avail itself of the working capital safe harbor; and (ii) meet the tangible property holding period requirement if at least 70-percent of its assets consist of QOZBP.

To the extent that ManagerCo is issued a profits interest under OpCo's operating agreement in exchange for services (or at the ManagerCo level to a member), such interests will not be treated as qualified interests and any subsequent gains with respect to such interests will be taxable.

## Step 4: Capitalizing the QOF (April 30, 2019)

The Investors will contribute $100 million of cash (or property) to the QOFs on April 30, 2019 in exchange for a preferred interest entitling such investors to an 8% preferred return and 60% of the residual profits thereafter.  ManagerCo will be entitled to the remaining 40% residual profits as to its promote interest.

The QOFs (InvestCo and ManagerCo) will contribute the $100M of cash invested by the Investors to OpCO (the QOZB) in exchange for all of the membership interests of OpCo.  The preferred return and promote will be reflected in OpCo's operating agreement.

## Step 5: Satisfy Initial Working Capital Requirements (May 2019)

A QOF must meet certain requirements in order to utilize the working capital safe harbor (allowing a QOZB to hold cash or equivalents for up to 31 months without such assets being treated as nonqualifying property).

First, the QOF must designate in writing that such working capital amounts are for the development of a trade or business in a QOZ, including when appropriate the acquisition, construction and/or substantial improvement of tangible property in such zone.

Second, the QOF must prepare a written schedule consistent with the ordinary start-up of a trade or business for the expenditure of the working capital assets. Under the schedule, the working capital assets must be spent within 31 months of the receipt by the business of such assets.

Third, the working capital assets must be actually used in a manner that is substantially consistent with the development plan and schedule described above. Importantly, if use of the working capital assets is delayed due to governmental inaction on a completed application, the delay does not cause a failure to meet the qualified property tests (which may extend the requirement to spend the working capital assets past 31 months).

## Step 6: Acquire Property by Purchase or Lease (May 15, 2019)

A QOZB then acquires property by purchase or lease (the property must have been acquired after December 31, 2017). Acquisition of property from a 20% or greater related person will not be treated as qualified property, but leases from a related party, are permitted subject to certain anti-abuse rules.

The QOZB will borrow $200 million (pursuant to a construction loan typical for such Project).

Under our facts, we assume that the QOZB uses $100 million of cash to acquire land and buildings. We assume that $60 million is properly allocable to the buildings and personal property, and the remaining $40 million is allocable to raw land.

## Step 7: Satisfy Original Use or Substantial Improvement Test (May 15, 2019 - November 15, 2021)

A QOF must satisfy either the original use test or the substantial improvement test. In order to be treated as qualified property, either the original use of such property must commence with the QOF or the property must be substantially improved by the QOF (as explained below).

## Original Use

Property may be treated as qualified property (subject to the acquisition and substantially all requirements) if the original use commences with the establishment of the QOF in a QOZ. If property (new or used) is first placed in service for purposes of depreciation or amortization with the QOF, it will meet the original use test. Likewise, property that was unused or vacant for an uninterrupted period of at least five years will be treated as original use property by the QOF. Used property that has not been previously used in a QOZ will meet the original use requirement. If used property had previously been used in an opportunity zone, it must be substantially improved by the QOF in order to be treated as qualified property.

## Substantial Improvement

A QOF (and QOZB) must substantially improve the acquired property by making an investment equal in value to the cost of the tangible property that is acquired by the QOF. Land is excluded for purposes of calculating substantial improvement. Thus, if a QOF acquires land and building for $100 million, with $40 million of the purchase price allocable to land and $60 million allocable to a building, the QOF is required to make improvements to the property of at least $60 million (equal to the acquisition basis of the building).

Under our facts, the QOZB owns the property and will use the $200 million construction loan proceeds to construct the Project (consisting of residential and commercial rental property).

In large part, leveraged real estate development projects will be constructed on newly acquired land and vacant buildings. Thus, the substantial improvement tests will likely not apply in such circumstances. Development projects should have little problem meeting the substantial improvement requirements (since the construction costs typically exceed the non-land cost by a significant margin). Major renovation projects may also satisfy the substantial improvement requirements. At the margin, the opportunity zone program could substantiate a broader rehabilitation or redevelopment in certain circumstances where expected construction would otherwise enable the developer to nearly, but not quite, meet the substantial improvement thresholds.

## Step 8: Satisfy Working Capital Safe Harbor (April 30, 2019 through November 30, 2021)

The QOF must first satisfy the initial working capital requirements described in Step 5 above (*e.g.*, preparing a business plan and budget). Thereafter, the QOF may avail itself of the working capital safe harbor. Under this safe harbor, cash, cash equivalents and debt instruments with a term of 18 months or less will not be counted towards the testing requirements (described below) for the 31 month period following the receipt of such funds (from any source) by the business. Thus, cash and qualifying financial property will not disqualify a QOF from meeting the requirement that the QOF hold qualified tangible property.

Funds that call capital (or borrow funds) at different times will have multiple 31 month periods to utilize the working capital safe harbor. The requirements above must be completed with respect to each separate receipt of funds by the QOF or an operating subsidiary.

## Step 9: First Testing Period (October 1, 2019)

On October 1, 2019 (the 6-month anniversary of QOF formation), each of the QOFs must test its assets in accordance with the 90-percent test. The sole asset of each QOF consists of the membership interests in OpCo. So long as OpCo is considered a QOZB, 100% of the QOF's interests in the

QOZB is considered qualified property, which will satisfy the 90-percent test for each QOF.

During the testing period (the first six-month period of the QOF's existence), OpCo must qualify as a QOZB in order for the QOF to meet the 90-percent test. OpCo's assets consisted of contributed cash, borrowed cash, land and building acquired on May 15, and any improvements to the land made during the testing period. However, all cash that is contributed during the prior six-month period (from April 1 to September 30, 2019) is excluded from the calculation. During the working capital safe harbor period, the entity is deemed to meet the tangible property test (regardless of the tangible property ratio). Likewise, since the QOZB is eligible for the working capital safe harbor, cash, cash equivalents and short term debt obligations will be excluded from the calculation for the 31 month period beginning as of the date of receipt of cash or property. Therefore, so long as OpCo otherwise meets the QOZB requirements for active conduct of a trade or business, use of intangible property and no 'sin' businesses, OpCo will be treated as a QOZB.

**Step 10: Second Testing Period (December 31, 2019)**

On December 31, 2019, each of the QOFs must test its assets in accordance with the 90-percent test (for the period from October 1, 2019 through December 31, 2019). The sole asset of each QOF consists of the membership interests in OpCo. So long as OpCo is considered a QOZB, each QOF will satisfy the 90-percent test.

**Step 11: Self-Certify as a QOF (March 15, 2020)**

On or before March 15, 2020 (or September 15, 2020 if the QOF filed an extension), each QOF will file their respective partnership tax returns (Form 1065) and file, with its tax return, Form 8896 to self-certify as a QOF effective April 2019. The QOF will also need to make sure that its organizing documents reflect its purposes to invest in QOZP. Finally, Form 8996 will reflect the results of the 90-percent testing requirements.

## Step 12: Permanent Financing (December 2021)

After construction of the project is complete, the QOZB will refinance the existing construction loan with permanent financing (assuming that the property is stabilized). Often, the permanent financing will provide sufficient excess cash to pay the preferred return to investors and, in some circumstances, repay a portion of the original invested capital to investors.

The QOZ rules explicitly permit a cash out refinance using debt financed distributions (so long as the recipient has sufficient basis resulting from its share of liabilities, which normally is the case for 2 years after all contributions). In most leveraged real estate fund investments, investors will be allocated a share of the partnership's debt which will be sufficient to receive debt financed distributions tax free.

## Step 13: Ongoing Operations (December 2021 through May 1, 2029)

In general, the QOFs and the QOZB will be operated in the same manner as a traditional leveraged real estate investment. Thus, the investors will, effectively, have the same tax treatment and economic returns as they would be entitled to in the absence of the QOZ program.

Each QOF will continue to test its assets every six-month period and file Form 8996 with its partnership tax return to reflect its qualifications as a QOF and to determine any penalties for failure to meet the asset tests, as well as the other requirements to be treated as a QOZB.

To the extent that a subsequent capital contribution is made: (1) in order to obtain the QOZ tax incentives, it must be made with reinvested capital gains to be treated as an eligible investment; and (2) a new holding period begins with respect to such subsequent investment. This is also starts the clock for debt financed distributions within 2 years.

## Step 14: Gain Recognition for Investors (December 31, 2026)

From the perspective of the QOF, the December 31, 2026 "inclusion date" (which is the last day that any invested capital gains will be recognized by the investor if not previously recognized) does not create any obligation on behalf of a QOF. However, the investors of the QOF will recognize their original capital gains (subject to basis adjustments, as applicable) and will owe tax. In some cases, it may be ideal to refinance near this time frame and distribute cash to investors so that they have cash to pay the tax liability on the original deferred gain.

In unprofitable deals, the investor would benefit by including in income the fair market value of their investment, less basis (instead of the remaining deferred gain). Thus, the QOF may assist investors to coordinate valuations (which will reduce costs and possibly, the risk that the valuation would be challenged).

## Step 15: Disposition After 10 Years (June 1, 2029)

On June 1, 2029, the property will be sold for $600 million. After repayment of debt (approximately $147 million) and payment of transaction costs (approximately $20 million), the balance of $433 million will be distributed to the partners in accordance with the respective operating agreements of the QOF and its subsidiary entities. To the extent that the refinance at the time of permanent financing and cash flow from operations covered the payment for preferred return (but not the principal), the distribution to partners at the time of the sale will be approximately (i) $100 million return of invested capital to preferred members; (ii) $200 million to preferred members (equal to 60% of residual cash flow) and (iii) $133 million with respect to the promote interest (equal to 40% of residual cash flow). Thus, the project generated a pre-tax return for the investors of 16.61% (calculated using the Excel XIRR formula).

To the extent that the property (consisting of personal property, qualified improvements, residential rental property and commercial rental property) was depreciated from $300 million to $100 million, the investors have capital account balances of negative $100 million. Thus, the sale of the property (under normal tax rules) for $600 million would generate taxable gain of $680 million (after taking into account transaction expenses). Of this amount, $200 million consists of depreciation recapture (assumed to be §1250 gain taxed an aggregate federal and state tax rate of 37%) and the remainder is capital gain (taxed at an aggregate federal and state tax rate of 32%). Accordingly, the estimated federal and state tax liability resulting from the sale if no election is made will be $228 million.

The QOF must carefully structure its sale to allow its investors to maximize their tax benefits. A sale of QOF equity interests will allow for the investors to step up the basis to fair market value (and a corresponding inside basis step up will be made by the QOF), resulting in no gain or loss (even with respect to the QOF's share of nonqualified assets and ordinary income assets other than inventories).

If a QOF sells its assets, the taxpayer will exclude any capital gain from the disposition with respect to its qualified investment. In a leveraged real estate transaction, these two approaches will likely have very similar outcomes.

# PLANNING IDEAS FOR A LEVERAGED REAL ESTATE QOF

### Timing Investor Contributions

In a typical real estate fund, capital is called as required for investment into new projects (typically at the time of land acquisition for development projects with the balance derived from construction loans). This structure is problematic since investors must use capital gains to invest into a fund in order to qualify for the tax benefits. Accordingly, alternative structures must be considered.

One approach is that funds may be raised on a project by project basis. This is inefficient from a capital raise perspective, but solves the problem of having investors with potential for disallowed gains.

In some cases, the fund could have all capital contributed up front, even if projects are not yet ready to go. This is potentially costly for the fund (if the investors will be paid a preferred return on invested capital) but allows for all investors to ensure that they will be able to defer capital gains.

A QOF may require cash up front that exceeds the investor's current availability of eligible gains. This problem may be solved using convertible debt. A fund could structure its investment as a convertible note that is convertible at the initial fair market value and returns a coupon that is equivalent to the preferred return. The investor could then convert its debt into equity at any time which would allow the investor to control the timing of the investment of gains. Note, however, that the 10 year holding period would not begin until the time that such conversion was made and the economic rights of the equity holders and debt holders may differ (at least in regard to residual allocations of profits and/or cash flows).

### General Structuring Matters

As is detailed in various sections of this book, most QOFs will be structured with two or more separate partnerships or other entities (which may be treated as QOFs) that in turn own equity interests in a QOZB. The two-tier structure is required for most projects so that the QOZB can utilize the working capital safe harbor and the 70-percent qualifying asset test (instead of 90-percent).

Since restructuring a QOF is not particularly easy (as many transactions would cause inclusion events), the manner in which a QOF and QOZB are structured up-front will have tax ramifications upon disposition. A properly structured fund could allow for a mechanism by with investors holding qualifying investments will be able to sell equity rather than utilize the asset election to exclude gain. This approach may not be necessary in the context of a leveraged real estate fund (since ordinary income may be negligible and the fund may not hold any nonqualifying assets that are sold at a gain). However, the sale of equity would eliminate any potential for such tax inefficiencies.

## Tax Treatment of Promote and Profits Interests

Profits interests are not eligible for the tax benefits under the QOZ program. To the extent that a sponsor has a promote interest that is part capital interest and part profits interest, the non-qualifying portion is generally based on the highest residual profit percentage attributable to the profits or promote interests.

In some cases, the promote interest increases after certain IRR hurdles are achieved. The literal reading of the Regulations require that the promote interest holder treats the portion of its interest as non-qualifying based on the highest percentage interest attributable to the profits or promote interest (that is reasonably attainable). This rule could artificially increase the share of interests that are non-qualifying. Thus, an investor that also receives a promote interest may benefit from having its capital interest issued to one taxpayer and the profits interest issued to a separate taxpayer (with common indirect ownership).

Moreover, it is not clear whether the equity structure of a business may be designed to allow for a sponsor to acquire a speculative equity interest for cash rather than receive a profits interest. For example, a sponsor could receive fee income that properly compensates the sponsor for services, and acquire residual interests that are comparable to the risky tranches of a bond fund or CDO for cash.

Alternatively, an upper-tier profits interest may be issued to a partner that itself is an investor in a QOF.

### Substantial Improvements of Property

In the context of a development project, meeting the substantial improvement requirement is often not very difficult (since there is no requirement to improve land, and the value attributable to land is excluded from the calculation). In some cases, however, meeting the substantial improvement requirement will be difficult if it involves rehabilitation of structures.

In such a circumstance, a taxpayer would benefit with a larger allocation to land. To avoid the risk that the tax benefits of a QOF would be eliminated, any such allocations may be supported by an appraisal to reduce the risk that the QOF would be deemed to fail the substantial improvement test.

### Valuation Matters at December 31, 2026

QOFs and QOZBs may benefit from the "lesser of" rule that requires an investor to recognize as of any inclusion date or December 31, 2026 (subject to basis adjustments), the remaining deferred gain (or proportion thereof) or the fair market value of the investment at such time. The fair market value of equity interests in an operating business may be lower than the value as of the date of investment. The taxable gain rule applicable to partnerships is also base don the fair market value of the investment as of such date.

In certain types of funds, this effect is more prevalent. For example, a fund could return capital to a preferred investor without limiting such investor's potential upside (such that equity is not considered reduced at the time that the capital is repaid in part). Market fluctuations could then cause the investor's equity to have decreased when valued as of December 31, 2026. Moreover, contractual arrangements may create substantial additional discounts that are appropriate for determining the fair market value of the equity interest as of December 31, 2026 (*e.g.*, a permanent loan may be subject to onerous prepayment penalties or defeasance costs and may contain restrictions on the use of funds, the fund could prohibit transfers (or require an offer of the interests to the fund)).

In such a case, the investor may reduce gain with respect to the original deferred gain while continuing to own the equity interests. If the equity interests are subsequently sold (years later) at a large gain, the investor will have eliminated some amount of tax on both the original deferred gain and the appreciation of the investment.

To the extent that equity interests in the fund would be valued at fair market value (reducing the deferred gain), the fund may be able to assist its investors to reduce costs by coordinating a valuation from an intendent third party valuation firm. This may also reduce risk for the investor group since the larger group's reliance (and sign off of their respective advisors) provides legitimacy to the conclusion of value.

Note that a leveraged real estate fund (that is sensitive to its investor's cash needs) may try to time a cash out refinance in a manner to provide cash for investors to cover their potential tax obligation.

# CHAPTER FOUR

# Opportunity Zones for Business Owners

Benefiting from opportunity fund investments in the operating business context is unpredictable. Real estate investments allow for relatively predictable cash flows, and benefit from an extremely robust market that allows for virtually all real estate to attract ready buyers (without significant cost) for sale at reasonable market prices.[15] An operating business, on the other hand, is much less predictable with respect to operating cash flows and the ability to sell at a particular point in time. Thus, an operating business' ability to benefit from the QOZ program is not assured. Indeed, we have referred to the use of a QOF structure for an operating business as buying a "lottery ticket" since it requires the confluence of a number of unlikely factors

Nevertheless, the function of the QOZ for an operating business is effectively identical to that for leveraged real estate. The following steps reflect the life cycle of an operating business QOF and the consequences. For purposes of consistency, we have used an example that is economically similar to the prior scenarios.

Note that many of the steps and planning tips are substantially similar to those set forth in Chapter 3 since the compliance for real estate and operating business activities is subject to the same general rules.

## LIFE CYCLE OF A BUSINESS QOF (FROM THE PERSPECTIVE OF A BUSINESS OWNER OR SPONSOR)

Assume that the proposed investment requires that investors (collectively) invest $100 million into a QOF in exchange for a membership interest that provides for an 8% preferred return on unreturned invested capital (compounded annually) and 60% of all residual profits after payment of the preferred return. The remaining 40% of the residual profits (after payment of the preferred return) is the sponsor's promote interest. The $100 million investment will be used to fund research and development for a software technology platform. The investment will close (*i.e.*, the funds will be contributed) on April 30, 2019. We further assume that the company will be sold on May 1, 2029 for $400 million.

### Step 1: Preliminary Activities (January 1, 2018 through April 30, 2019)

Often, a start-up business will engage in business activities prior to its initial capital raise. In this stage, a technology development company will often engage in formation and legal structuring, prepare a business plan and create a proof of concept with respect to the proposed technology.

Business assets developed prior to the formation of a QOF will not be qualified assets. Such assets will need to be contributed, leased/licensed or sold to the QOF following formation. In a typical (i.e., non-QOZ) arrangement, the founder would contribute such assets to the operating business (so that the investors have rights without limitation on valuable intellectual property). The contribution of such assets could result in a mixed fund investment for the contributor.

Thus, it may make sense for the business founder to *sell* all of the assets to the newly formed QOF after its formation and then contribute the cash received back (from such sale) to the QOF (this could be built into the economic arrangement).[16] Alternatively, such assets could be leased under a long term lease, which has the effect of freezing the current value of such assets that do not obtain QOZ benefits since the lease effectively locks in today's value.

## Step 2: Capital Raising Activities (January 1, 2018 through April 30, 2019)

Once the proof of concept is complete, the sponsor must line up capital. However, in this context, the developer or sponsor must cause the investors to contribute capital that consists of capital gains recognized by such investor during the applicable 180-day timeframe (if such investors intend to benefit from opportunity zones).

## Step 3: Structuring the QOF (April 2019)

The sponsor will structure the business in order to maximize the tax benefits under the QOZ program and form the respective entities (including the QOF or QOFs). In this regard, the sponsor will form three limited liability companies that will be treated as partnerships for tax purposes. The following structure chart reflects the general structure (which is identical to the structure for the leveraged real estate example used in Chapter 3).

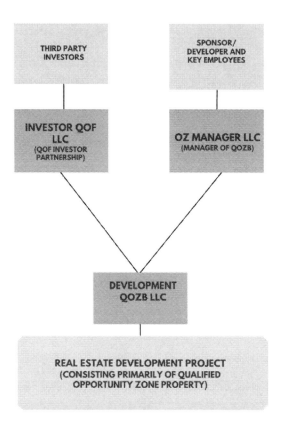

The operating business is treated as a QOZ partnership interest. Accordingly, the operating business may avail itself of the working capital safe harbor and meet the tangible property holding period requirement if at least 70-percent of its assets consist of QOZBP.

Investor QOF LLC ("InvestCo") and OZ Manager LLC ("ManagerCo") are the owners of Development QOZB LLC ("OpCo"). InvestCo will be treated as a QOF. ManagerCo will normally not be treated as a QOF since it receives a carried interest and QOF treatment would be inefficient (any contributions by the developer should be made through a separate QOF).

The organizational documents for InvestCo will include a provision providing that the QOF was formed for the purpose of investing in QOZP.

Note that the QOF should determine whether OpCo may benefit from being treated as a qualified small business corporation (which may be sold after a five-year holding period with 100% of gain excluded up to certain thresholds). This approach is commonly used for venture funds and may likewise be appropriate for certain QOF businesses.

To the extent that ManagerCo is issued a profits interest under OpCo's operating agreement in exchange for services (or at the ManagerCo level to a member), such interests will not be treated as qualified interests and any subsequent gains with respect to such interests will be taxable.

## Step 4: Capitalizing the QOF (April 30, 2019)

The investors will contribute $100 million of cash (or property) to the QOFs on April 30, 2019 in exchange for a preferred interest entitling such investors to an 8% preferred return and 60% of the residual profits thereafter. ManagerCo will be entitled to the remaining 40% residual as its promote interest.

The QOFs will contribute the $100M of cash to OpCO (the QOZB) in exchange for all of the membership interests of OpCo. The preferred return and promote will be reflected in OpCo's operating agreement (or in either or both of the QOF operating agreements, as appropriate).

## Step 5: Satisfy Initial Working Capital Requirements (May 2019)

A QOF must meet certain requirements in order to utilize the working capital safe harbor (allowing a QOZB to hold cash or equivalents for up to 31 months without such assets being treated as nonqualifying property).

First, the QOF must reflect that such working capital amounts are designated in writing for the development of a trade or business in a QOZ, including when appropriate the acquisition, construction and/or substantial improvement of tangible property (which may be real or personal property) in such zone.

Second, the QOF must prepare a written schedule consistent with the ordinary start-up of a trade or business for the expenditure of the working capital assets. Under the schedule, the working capital assets must be spent within 31 months of the receipt by the business of such assets.

Third, the working capital assets must actually be used in a manner that is substantially consistent with the development plan and schedule described above. Please note that if use of the working capital assets is delayed due to governmental inaction on a completed application, the delay does not cause a failure (*i.e.*, extends the time) to meet the qualified property tests. In the context of an operating business, the extension of time may apply based on applications for approvals made to the FDA (in the case of medical device or biotechnology companies) or other governmental approvals in the case of any regulated business.

### Step 6: Acquire Property by Purchase or Lease (May 15, 2019)

A QOZB may acquire property by purchase *or* lease (the property must have been acquired after December 31, 2017). Leases from a related party, however, are permitted subject to certain anti-abuse rules. Note that the acquisition of property from a 20% or greater related person will not be treated as qualified property.

Under our facts, we assume that the QOZB uses $100 million of cash to fund the development of a technology platform. The business will likely spend only a relatively small proportion of the contributed capital on purchasing tangible property (which would consistent of leasehold improvements, computer equipment, software and office equipment). Other tangible property (such as real estate) would likely be leased by the company. The remainder of the funds would be set aside for research and development (primarily comprised of compensation for employees and payments to third-party independent contractors). This point reflects that the capital that is raised is not required to be spent on tangible property, so long as the other criteria to satisfy the QOZ program tests are met.

## Step 7: Satisfy Original Use or Substantial Improvement Test (May 15, 2019 through November 15, 2021)

A QOF must satisfy either the original use test or the substantial improvement test. In order to be treated as qualified property, either the original use of such property must commence with the QOF or the property must be substantially improved by the QOF.

### Original Use

Property may be treated as qualified property (subject to the acquisition and substantially all requirements) if the original use commences with the QOF in a QOZ. If property (new or used) is first placed in service for purposes of depreciation or amortization with the QOF, it will meet the original use test. Likewise, property that was unused or vacant for an uninterrupted period of at least five years will be treated as original use property by the QOF. Used property that has not been previously used in a QOZ will meet the original use requirement. Note that if used property had previously been used in the opportunity zone, it must be substantially improved by the QOF or it will not be treated as qualifying property.

For most operating businesses, the original use test will allow such businesses to satisfy these tests, as most of the property acquired will be new tangible equipment, furniture and fixtures that is acquired by the QOF or QOZB.

## Substantial Improvement

A QOF (and QOZB) must substantially improve the acquired property by making an investment equal to the cost of the tangible property that is acquired by the QOF. Many operating businesses will not acquire used equipment and the substantial improvement test will be inapplicable. Indeed, operating businesses that intend to qualify as a QOF or QOZB should not acquire (by purchase) used equipment that will not be improved since such property would not be qualifying property under the QOZ program (and such property could cause penalties or even the failure to meet the qualifications).

## Step 8: Satisfy Working Capital Safe Harbor (April 30, 2019 through November 30, 2021)

The QOF must first satisfy the initial working capital requirements described in Step 5 above (which effectively requires the QOF to document its business plan for the use of funds). Thereafter, the QOF may avail itself of the working capital safe harbor. Under this rule, cash, cash equivalents and debt instruments with a term of 18 months or less will not be counted towards the testing requirements (described below) for the 31-month period following the receipt of such funds (from any source) by the business.

Funds that call capital (or borrow funds) at different times will have a maximum of two 31-month periods (for a total of 62-months for start up companies) to utilize the working capital safe harbor. The requirements above (reflecting the written plan and use of funds) must be completed with respect to each separate receipt of funds by the QOF or an operating subsidiary.

## Step 9: First Testing Period (October 1, 2019)

On October 1, 2019 (the 6-month anniversary of QOF formation), each of the QOFs must test its assets in accordance with the 90-percent test (requiring at least 90-percent of its assets to be treated as QOZBP). The sole asset of each QOF consists of the membership interests in OpCo. So long as OpCo is considered a QOZB, each QOF will satisfy the 90-percent test.

During the testing period, OpCo must qualify as a QOZB in order for the QOF to meet the 90-percent asset test. The QOZB, in turn, must meet the 70-percent test (requiring that at least 70-percent of its assets qualify as QOZBP). OpCo's assets consisted of contributed cash, office and computer equipment, leasehold improvements, and any developed software that is appropriately capitalized. However, all cash that is contributed during the prior six-month period is excluded from the calculation. Likewise, since the QOZB is eligible for the working capital safe harbor, it is deemed to meet the tangible property test and cash, cash equivalents and short term debt obligations will be excluded from the calculation for the 31 month period beginning as of the date of receipt of cash or property.

For this business, the QOZB must ensure that it meets the gross income test (such that at least 50% of its gross income is derived from the active conduct of a trade or business in a QOZ). In the case of a software development business, this will likely be satisfied under the Hours or Compensation test if the work is being performed in a QOZ. Likewise, the QOZB should be able to satisfy the requirement that at least 40% of the intangible assets of the business are used in the active conduct of the trade or business since, under our facts, all intangible assets are used in the trade or business.

Thus, so long as 70-percent of the balance of OpCo's assets consist of qualified property (and OpCo otherwise meets the QOZB requirements for active conduct of trade or business, use of intangible property and no 'sin' businesses), OpCo will be treated as a QOZB.

## Step 10: Second Testing Period (December 31, 2019)

On December 31, 2019, each of the QOFs must test its assets in accordance with the 90-percent test. The sole asset of each QOF consists of the membership interests in OpCo. So long as OpCo is considered a QOZB, each QOF will satisfy the 90-percent test.

## Step 11: Self-Certify as a QOF (March 15, 2020)

On or before March 15, 2020 (or September 15, 2020 if the QOF filed an extension), each QOF will file their respective partnership tax returns (Form 1065) and file, with its tax return, Form 8896 to self-certify as a QOF effective April 2019. The QOF will also reflect that its organizing documents reflect its purposes to invest in QOZP. Finally, Form 8996 will reflect the results of the 90-percent testing requirements.

## Step 12: Ongoing Operations (December 2021 through May 1, 2029)

In general, the QOFs and the QOZB will be operated in the same manner as a traditional software development company each year. Thus, the investors will, effectively, have the same tax treatment and economic returns as they would be entitled to in the absence of the QOZ program (excluding the specific tax benefits under §1400Z-2).

To the extent that a subsequent capital contribution is made: (i) it must be made with reinvested capital gains to be treated as an eligible investment to obtain the QOZ tax incentives; and (ii) a new holding period begins with respect to such subsequent investment.

Each QOF will continue to test its assets every six-month period (after the working capital safe harbor period has expired) and file Form 8996 with its partnership tax return to reflect its qualifications as a QOF and to determine any penalties for failure to meet the asset tests, as well as the other requirements to be treated as a QOZB.

## Step 13: Gain Recognition for Investors (December 31, 2026)

From the perspective of the QOF, the December 31, 2026 inclusion date does not create any obligation on behalf of a QOF. However, the investors of the QOF will recognize their original capital gains (subject to basis adjustments, as applicable) and will owe tax.

In unsuccessful deals, the investor would benefit by including in income the fair market value of their investment, less basis (instead of the remaining deferred gain). Thus, the QOF may assist investors to coordinate valuations (which will reduce costs and possibly, the risk that the valuation would be challenged.

In the context of a software development business, if the developed software is not yet producing revenues and/or profits, it is possible that the company will be valued at a low valuation. In that case, the investors may only recognize a fraction of the original deferred gain.

## Step 14: Disposition After 10 Years (June 1, 2029)

On June 1, 2029, the property will be sold for $400 million. After payment of transaction costs (approximately $10 million), the balance of $390 million will be distributed to the partners in accordance with the respective operating agreements of the QOF and its subsidiary entities. To the extent that cash flow from operations covered the payment for preferred return (but not the principal), the distribution to partners at the time of the sale will be approximately (i) $100 million return of invested capital to preferred members; (ii) $174 million to preferred members (equal to 60% of residual cash flow) and (iii) $116 million with respect to the promote interest (equal to 40% of residual cash flow).

The QOF must carefully structure its sale to allow its investors to maximize their tax benefits. A sale of QOF equity interests will allow for the investors to step up the basis to fair market value (and a corresponding inside basis step up will be made by the QOF), resulting in no gain or loss, even with respect to the share of nonqualified assets and ordinary income assets.

## PLANNING IDEAS FOR BUSINESS OWNERS

### Coordination with Qualified Small Business Stock Incentives

Many venture investments are structured using qualified small business stock ("QSBS") which provides for tax-free gains on the disposition of QSBS that is held for at least 5 years. A qualified small business ("QSB") is a C corporation with $50 million or less in gross assets (at the time that the stock was issued) that engages in an active trade or business (with certain businesses excluded). The rationale for using a QSB as a vehicle for venture investing is that gains from the disposition of QSBS, if held for at least 5 years, will be tax-free up to the lesser of 10 times the adjusted basis in the stock or $10 million.

A QOF or QOZB may be structured as a QSB.

The net effect of combining these approaches is that:

1.  The investor may defer *any* capital gains under the QOZ program (under the QSB tax incentive, gains from the sale of QSBS may only be deferred if reinvested in another QSB).

2.  If the investor disposes of stock in the QSB after 5 years, but prior to 10 years, the investor will still receive at least partial tax-free gain treatment. If the stock is held for 10 years, the entire gain will be tax free under the QOZ program.

In the context of venture fund investing, the use of a C corporation structure for underlying investments is preferred by many institutional investors (primarily for compliance reasons, and due to the tax rules for tax-exempt entities).

Note that many businesses will benefit, on an after-tax basis, using a pass-through (*i.e.*, partnership) structure. For such businesses, the use of QSBS will not be the preferred structure.

## Building Intangible Value in a Zone Entity

Closely held businesses are typically sold using actual or deemed asset sales. When the assets of a business are sold, the primary value is considered "goodwill" which generally represents the value of the intangible assets of a business (*i.e.*, brand, marks, customer list, reputation, processes, know-how, etc.).

Building the goodwill value inside of an opportunity zone is easy for businesses that solely exist as a QOF or QOZB. However, businesses that grow may ultimately consist of a QOZ entity and a non-zone entity. In these situations, it is critical that a business understand how to build (and retain) goodwill value in QOZ.

For example, the initial intellectual property rights (such as brand name, trademarks, technology) are owned by the QOZ and QOZB (subject to the testing requirements for intangibles that are self-created). Reflecting value of such attributes is buttressed if the marketing, advertising, research and development, and corporate strategy personnel work from the QOZ entity.

The relationship between a QOZ entity and non-QOZ entity are also important. The non-zone entities should have a very specific purpose, with limited upside potential (this may be accomplished through such entity acting as a licensee or franchisee of the zone entity).

Ultimately, upon disposition of a businesses, the various assets and/or equity interests of entities will be valued by the buyer and seller. The facts will govern the value in the zone entity as compared to a non-zone entity. By planning early, a business should be able to maximize the value of the QOF or QOZB as compared to non-zone entities. Ultimately, this approach will greatly reduce taxation (and increase the after-tax return for investors).

## Tax Treatment of Promote and Profits Interests

Profits interests are not eligible for the tax benefits under the QOZ program. To the extent that a sponsor has a promote interest that is part capital interest and part profits interest, the non-qualifying portion is based on the highest residual profit percentage attributable to the profits or promote interests.

In some cases, the promote interest increases after certain IRR hurdles are achieved. The Regulations generally requires that the promote interest holder treats the portion of its interest as non-qualifying based on the highest percentage interest attributable to the profits or promote interest. This rule could artificially increase the share of interests that are non-qualifying. Thus, an investor that also receives a promote interest may benefit from having its capital interest issued to one taxpayer and the profits interest issued to a separate taxpayer (with common ownership).

Moreover, it is not clear whether the equity structure of a business may be designed to allow for a sponsor to acquire a speculative equity interest for cash rather than receive a profits interest. For example, a sponsor could receive fee income that properly compensates the sponsor for services, and acquire residual interests that are comparable to the risky tranches of a bond fund or CDO for cash.

Alternatively, an upper-tier profits interest may be issued to a partner that itself is an investor in a QOF.

## Structuring Dispositions

An investor may elect to exclude income (resulting from an asset sale) solely with respect to capital gains from the disposition of qualified property. The asset sale election therefore will require the investors to recognize taxable income with respect to the disposition of certain ordinary income assets (*e.g.,* inventories). Note that in the context of real estate, these issues may not be problematic; they could certainly arise in the context of the sale of an operating business.

The effect of this rule is that the disposition of a QOF or QOZB necessitates a structure to allow for the sale of membership interests or stock rather the sale of underlying assets. The fact pattern of a particular business and industry (as well as the relationship and intent of the investor owners) are relevant to determine how such interests could be properly structured.

## Valuation Matters at December 31, 2026

Operating business QOFs and QOZBs may benefit from the "lesser of" rule that requires an investor to recognize as of any inclusion date or December 31, 2026 (subject to basis adjustments), the remaining deferred gain (or proportion thereof) or the fair market value of the investment at such time. The fair market value of equity interests in an operating business may be lower than the value as of the date of investment.

In certain types of businesses, this effect is more prevalent. For example, a business that remains in the development stage (*i.e.*, pre-revenue) may be valued (by a certified valuation analyst) on December 31, 2026 at a very low value. In such a case, the investor may reduce or eliminate gain entirely with respect to the original deferred gain while continuing to own the equity interests. If the equity interests are subsequently sold (years later) at a large gain, the investor will have effectively eliminated (or nearly eliminated) tax on both the original deferred gain and the appreciation of the investment.

# Part 2

# Analysis for Tax and Legal Professionals

CHAPTER FIVE

# Framework of the Qualified Opportunity Zone Program

The qualified opportunity zone legislation passed under the 2017 tax act (commonly referred to as the Tax Cut and Jobs Act, or "TCJA") allows taxpayers to defer gains that are reinvested in certain investment vehicles. After recognizing such deferred gains by 2026, the taxpayer may ultimately dispose of their investment tax-free. The qualified opportunity zone program combines specific policy objectives of investing in lower-income communities with tax objectives that target multiple stakeholders: investors, fund managers, developers and business owners.

The legislation consists of two separate statutes that, respectively, (1) designate certain geographic areas as "qualified opportunity zones" (sometimes referred to herein as a "QOZ" or "QOZs") and (2) provide for tax benefits in connection with an investment in a "qualified opportunity fund" ("QOF").

First, §1400Z-1 authorizes each State and the District of Columbia to designate up to 25-percent of low-income community census tracts (which consist of "low income communities", designated by census tracts meeting certain income-based criteria) in such jurisdiction as a "qualified opportunity zone".[17] The designation process was completed, and the zones finalized in June 2018.[18]

Second, the TCJA enacted the rules to enable an investment to qualify for the various tax benefits under §1400Z-2:

1. Tax Benefits for Investors. Under the opportunity zone program, investors will be able benefit from tax deferral (with respect to cash or property invested in a qualified entity) and tax reduction/elimination (accomplished through basis adjustments following statutory holding periods). The net effect of these tax benefits is to substantially increase the after-tax return for an investor in a QOF.

2. Requirements of a QOF. The statute reflects the structure and requirements of the entity that will serve as the investment vehicle (including the application to underlying business operations).

Since the QOZ designations are complete, the focus now relates to the availability of benefits for investors (relating to gain deferral, inclusion, and tax-free appreciation) and applicable funds (generally relating to structure, operational requirements, and compliance issues).

The QOZ program is based on the rules set forth in §1400Z-2 of the Internal Revenue Code and Regulations §§1.1400Z2(a)-(f).[19] The statute (and Regulations) reflect the five major components of the law:

- **Investment of Capital Gains**. What constitutes qualifying reinvested capital gains eligible for deferral?

- **Deferral and Inclusion of Gains**. When is gain deferred and when (and how much) deferred gain is included in income?

- **Tax-Free Dispositions After Ten Years**. How are taxable gains treated (and eliminated) for property disposed of following a ten-year holding period?

- **Formation and Structure of a Qualified Opportunity Fund**. What are the requirements of a qualified opportunity fund?

- **Other Rules and Compliance Matters**. Miscellaneous rules pertaining to mixed investments, related party rules, income in respect of a decedent, certification, and how opportunity fund profits may be reinvested.

The qualified opportunity zone legislation specifies four explicit, statutory tax benefits. Implicit in the statute (and in some cases, clarified under the Regulations), additional substantial tax benefits are applicable to investors in a QOF.

The tax benefits for an investor will generally consist of the following statutory tax benefits:

a. A taxpayer may **defer reinvested capital gains** until the date that is the earlier of (i) the date that the investment is sold or exchanged or (ii) December 31, 2026.[20]

b. After the investor has held its investment for 5 years, it is entitled to a **step-up in basis** equal to 10-percent of the original deferred gain.[21] In order to obtain this benefit, the investment must have been made by December 31, 2021.[22]

   c.  After the investor has held its investment for 7 years, it is entitled to another **step-up in basis** equal to an additional 5-percent of the original deferred gain (for a total of 15-percent).[23] In order to obtain this benefit, the investment must have been made by December 31, 2019.[24]

   d.  After the investor has held its investment for ten years, any capital gain resulting from the sale or exchange of such investment will be **tax-free gain** (which is accomplished through a basis adjustment to fair market value as of the date of the sale or exchange or an election to exclude capital gain).[25]

In some cases, an investor will benefit from the following tax benefits that are inherent in the structure of the program:

   a.  A taxpayer will **not recognize any depreciation recapture or trigger minimum gain** for properly structured investments held more than 10 years.

   b.  If the fair market value of the taxpayer's investment is less than the remaining deferred gain as of December 31, 2026, the taxpayer will **never recognize a portion of their remaining deferred gain**.[26]

The effect of the foregoing tax incentives is to greatly enhance the after-tax return on a taxpayer's investment in a QOF. Indeed, in many cases the after-tax internal rate of return ("IRR") for typical investment deals will be increased by 25-50% (based solely on the benefits under the opportunity zone program as compared to an identical investment without such tax benefits).[27] In the context of operating businesses, the tax benefits can be even more significant if the entire business is sold after a 10-year holding period.

# CHAPTER SIX

# Reinvestment of Capital Gains

The threshold requirement to obtain the opportunity zone tax benefits is that an investor must reinvest capital gains (*i.e.*, recognize capital gains, and within 180 days, invest such amount in a fund). Section 1400Z-2(a) provides that if a taxpayer (i) realizes gain from the sale to, or exchange with, an unrelated person, and (ii) invests such gain in a QOF during the 180-day period beginning on the date of such sale or exchange, the taxpayer may elect to defer such gain until the earlier of (a) the date that the investment is sold or exchanged or (b) December 31, 2026. In other words, a taxpayer will not recognize taxable gain (until 2026, in most cases) on the amount of eligible gain that is invested in a QOF.

The statute explicitly provides that investors will include the previously incurred gain as provided by the inclusion rules under §1400Z-2(b) and that qualifying investments held for over 10 years will be tax-free under §1400Z-2(c).[28]

The separate components of the statute (listed below) are discussed in detail in the following pages.

1. What is "gain" that qualifies for reinvestment?
2. What constitutes a "sale or exchange"?
3. Which related party rules apply (*i.e.*, what is an "unrelated person")?
4. How does a taxpayer make an election to defer gain?
5. What is a considered a 'taxpayer' eligible to make an election?
6. What constitutes an "investment"?
7. How is the 180-day period determined?
8. Reinvestment rules for QOFs

## WHAT GAINS WILL QUALIFY FOR REINVESTMENT?

### *Eligible Gains*

Section 1400Z-2(a) provides that "gain from the sale or exchange" may be deferred as provided in the statute. There is no reference to whether the gain may be long term or short term, ordinary or capital, or even whether it includes portfolio gains. The Regulations clarify this ambiguity by defining what constitutes an "eligible gain".[29] To be treated as eligible gain, such gain (A) must be treated as capital gain for income tax purposes (or is a qualified §1231 gain within the meaning of Reg. §1400Z-2(b)(11)(iii)(A), discussed below); (B) would be recognized for federal income tax purposes before January 1, 2027 if §1400Z-2 did not apply;[30] and (C) does not arise from a sale or exchange with a related person.[31]

Thus, a taxpayer may reinvest capital gains that are recognized on or before December 31, 2026. A taxpayer will have made a qualifying investment so long as the investment is made in a QOF on or before June 28, 2027.

The Regulations also clarify that eligible gain is determined without taking losses into account.[32] Accordingly, eligible gains include a taxpayer's gross amount of capital gains, expanding the pool of potential investors. Moreover, gain that is recharacterized as ordinary income is not eligible gain.[33]

If a taxpayer has already made an election to defer gain, such elected gain is no longer "eligible gain" (*i.e.*, a single gain cannot be treated as a qualifying gain twice, although a single (larger) gain can be spread among multiple QOF investments).[34] This rule is intended to explicitly prohibit a taxpayer from making multiple investments with the same gain, but not prohibit reinvestment of gain resulting from an inclusion event. Gains that arise from an inclusion event are eligible to be reinvested in a QOF (the same QOF or another QOF) so long as such gains otherwise qualify for reinvestment under the general QOZ rules.[35] Thus, the taxpayer will have 180 days from the date of the inclusion event to reinvest the gain and the holding period begins on the date that such gains are reinvested in a QOF.

*Planning Tip:* A taxpayer could inadvertently cause a mixed-inclusion if gains are reinvested in the same QOF that was subject to an earlier investment since the taxpayer would have different holding periods for the same QOF. This concern may be solved by making the new investment through a new QOF, or using a different investor entity (such as a partnership) that is treated as having its own holding period.

Under the definition of "eligible gains", the gains must be capital in nature, but will include both short- and long-term gains. The legislative history explicitly identifies "capital gains" as the gains that are eligible for deferral.[36]

Thus, the Regulations state that in order to be an eligible gain it must be "treated as capital gain for income tax purposes". Many types of gain are generally treated as capital gains, even when taxed at differing rates including: long and short term capital gains from the sale of capital assets; §1231 gain; unrecaptured §1250 gain;[37] and collectibles gains.[38] Types of gain that are characterized in the foregoing categories (such as §1256 gains) will also be treated as capital gains eligible for deferral. The nature of gain recognition is irrelevant; gains are eligible from an actual or deemed sale or exchange. Ultimately, any other gain (except as provided below) that is required to be included in the computation of capital gain will be eligible for reinvestment.

## §1231 Gains

Section 1231 gain is gain from the disposition of property (including real property) used in a trade or business (or gains resulting from involuntary conversions of certain property). Section 1231 gains are recognized under general tax principles only as of the last day of the taxable year (by netting all §1231 gains and §1231 losses of a taxpayer).[39] Under the Regulations, the §1231 gain, like regular non-business capital gain, is computed exclusive of the §1231 losses and without regard as to whether the gain should be treated as capital or ordinary under §1231. Fortunately, the Regulations eliminated the requirement to net §1231 gains and losses. The eligible gain is limited to the extent that it exceeds any amount that must be treated as ordinary income under §1245 or §1250, unreduced by §1231 losses. Otherwise, gross §1231 gains are eligible for reinvestment (in the same manner as regular capital gains).

Often, the delay to begin the "clock" until December 31 may be highly favorable. The treatment as capital gain outside of an entity (treated as occurring on the date of the sale) as compared to §1231 gain changes the timing requirements to begin the 180-day period significantly. **In many**

**cases, the rule applicable to §1231 gains will be helpful since it effectively gives a taxpayer the remainder of the year, plus 6 months to identify and make such investment (resulting in up to 18 months to reinvest the gains from the date of the underlying transaction).**

In many cases, the disposition of rental real estate or assets of a business will be treated as §1231 gain. The effect of this rule is to delay the taxpayer's ability to invest in a QOF until the following tax year. This could significantly delay reinvestment of the gain that would otherwise be invested early in the year (within 180 days of the transaction giving rise to the gain). Moreover, this causes issues with current investors that have §1231 gains from early 2019 and cannot reinvest until 2020 (in some cases, these funds may have already been earmarked for a specific investment under the assumption that §1231 gains would be eligible immediately for reinvestment). Fortunately, the IRS recognized this issue for early investors, and determined that §1231 gains that were reinvested prior to the end of the 2018 tax year will qualify for reinvestment based on the date of the transaction itself.[40]

Section 1231 losses incurred during the prior 5 years are subject to recapture. The effect of this rule is that §1231 gains in a subsequent tax year will be treated as ordinary income instead of capital gains up to the amount of carryover §1231 losses. For purposes of the QOZ program, it does not appear that the rules for current §1231 gains are affected by prior year §1231 losses (such that §1231 gains may be reinvested without recapture). In other words, a taxpayer may reinvest all of its §1231 gain for the year and the potential recapture of prior losses (and conversion to ordinary income) could be avoided if no §1231 gains are incurred during the remaining recapture period. If that is a correct interpretation of the rule, a taxpayer may be able to avoid recapture by investing §1231 gains from one year until the prior year §1231 losses have expired for purposes of calculating net §1231 gains – which has the effect of eliminating potential ordinary income permanently.

## §1256 Gains

Similarly, in the case of §1256 contracts, only the capital gain net income will be eligible for deferral for that year (which is determined by aggregating all of the taxpayer's §1256 gains and losses for the year) rather than each transaction being eligible independently.[41] Moreover, since the net gain from §1256 contracts can only be determined at the close of the tax year, the 180-day period begins on the last day of the tax year for the net gain resulting from §1256 contracts. The Regulations contain a restriction on the use of offsetting positions transactions (defined below) which provides that if a taxpayer engaged in *any* offsetting positions transactions with a §1256 contract and any other provision in that transaction was *not* a §1256 contract, then *no gain from any* §1256 contract will be eligible for deferral for that year.[42]

If capital gain arises from a position that is or has been part of an certain identified straddles, the gain is not eligible for deferral under §1400Z-2(a)(1).[43] In general, an offsetting-position transaction is a hedging transaction, including a straddle (as defined under §1092) or a position that would be a straddle if the straddle definition did not contain the active trading requirement in §1092(d)(1). An offsetting-positions transaction also includes a position in closely held stock or other non-traded personal property and substantially offsetting derivatives.

### Non-Eligible Gains: Deemed Gains Arising as a Result of §752 Liabilities

The Regulations prohibit the deferral of gain that was realized upon the shift of liabilities that resulted from the transfer (which is a deemed disposition) of property to a QOF in exchange for an eligible interest or the transfer of property to an eligible taxpayer for an eligible interest.[44] The effect of this prohibition is to disqualify gains resulting from a shift in §752 liabilities for deferral treatment, when the gain itself results from the investment in that QOF. This rule is consistent with the treatment of §752 liabilities for contribution purposes (*i.e.*, deemed contributions due to an assumption of liabilities by a partner will not be considered a contribution for purposes of determining an investor's contribution to a QOF).

### *Tax Attributes for Gain Inclusion*

To the extent that previously deferred gain is included in income, the gain at the time it is included is considered to have the same attributes as it would have had if the tax on the gain was not deferred.[45] Such attributes include those described in §1(h), §1222, §1256 and any other applicable provisions of the Code. Accordingly, the character of short-term capital gain, §1231 gain, §1256 gain, etc. will not change merely because the deferred gain is recognized in a subsequent tax year.

The federal income tax provisions and rates applicable in the inclusion year will apply when such gain is recognized.[46] Note that changes in tax rates may be detrimental. If rate increases are scheduled to occur, taxpayers may look for ways to create an inclusion event prior to December 31, 2026 (as to deferred capital gains) that does not impact the 10-year holding period in order to mitigate the impact of a pending rate increase.

The Regulations apply various rules to determine which eligible gain is included with a particular deferral election and a particular investment.[47] The taxpayer will generally rely on published IRS guidance and forms. However, if a deferred gain is not "clearly associated" with a particular qualifying investment, the rules under the Regulations will apply.

If only one gain could have been deferred with respect to a particular investment, then that deferred gain will be associated with that particular investment.[48] A general first-in first-out rule applies such that if more than one eligible gain is deferred with respect to an investment in a QOF, that the earliest investment is associated with the earliest realized eligible gain.[49] If two eligible gains are recognized on the same day, the gains are allocated to the investment in the QOF proportionately.

If a taxpayer acquired interests in a QOF stock with identical rights (referred to in the Regulations as "fungible interests"), but at different times, and such taxpayer disposes of some, but not all, of such interests on the same day, the taxpayer will use the first-in first-out ("FIFO") method to determine which interests were disposed of.[50] The FIFO method is used for three purposes under the Regulations: (A) to determine whether an investment was an eligible investment in a QOF or deemed to be made with mixed funds; (B) to identify the attributes of the investment at the time the gain is included in income; and (C) to calculate the extent, if any, of an increase in basis of such investment under §1400Z-2(b)(2)(B) when such investment is disposed of. The Regulations do not explicitly apply the FIFO rules to basis step up and dispositions under §1400Z-2(c). Thus, as drafted, the Regulations do not provide for FIFO treatment in determining tax free treatment for dispositions after 10 years. This omission potentially causes a partial sale of interests after 10 years as being partially taxable (when it would have been tax-free under the FIFO method).

Under traditional partnership tax rules, the disposition of an interest is treated as a proportionate disposition of the entire partnership interest (*i.e.,* a partner is deemed to hold a single partnership interest, with different holding periods based on the timing of the acquisition of such interests). The use of the FIFO method is therefore advantageous to taxpayers as compared to regular tax principles and will allow taxpayers to maximize the benefits under the QOZ program.

The Regulations adopt a pro rata method if the FIFO method is inapplicable.[51] In this regard, if, after the application of the FIFO method, a taxpayer is treated as having disposed of less than all of the investment interests that the taxpayer acquired one day and, if the interests that were so acquired on that day vary with respect to its characteristics, the proportionate allocation method must be made to determine which interests were disposed of.

The timing of gain inclusion has important state tax considerations (which are discussed in more detail in Chapter 12 below). Most states follow the Code as enacted under the TCJA. Some states have not yet adopted conformity with the TCJA but otherwise follow the Code.

*Practice Tip*: A taxpayer could defer the gain when such taxpayer resides in a high-tax state, and recognize the gain in a year in which the taxpayer resides in a low tax state.[52] Alternatively, The foregoing rules must be considered at the time that a taxpayer elects to defer any of its gains. If a taxpayer is in a low-income or zero tax bracket in the year of deferral (*e.g.*, taxpayer has a current net operating loss), it may benefit by deferring long term rather than short term gains (in order to take advantage of the lower rate when the gain is ultimately recognized).[53]

## WHAT CONSTITUTES A "SALE OR EXCHANGE"?

### General Rule

Section 1400Z-2(a)(1) provides that gain may be deferred resulting from "the sale to, or an exchange with" an unrelated person.[54] Although the term "sale or exchange" (or the past tense "sold or exchanged") is used throughout the statute and the Regulations, such term is not defined for purposes of §1400Z-2. Nonetheless, the term "sale or exchange" is commonly used for other purposes of the Code and the meaning of such term should likewise be applicable under the qualified opportunity zone legislation.

The preamble to the 2018 Proposed Regulations provides that eligible gains generally include "capital gain from an actual, or deemed, sale or exchange". Thus, for purposes of §1400Z-2, a sale or exchange refers to any actual or deemed sale or exchange of a capital asset that gives rise to capital gains. The Regulations note that non-sale or exchange transactions such as gifts, bequests, charitable contributions, and abandonments of qualifying investments are not considered sales or exchanges.

### Definition of "Sale or Exchange"

Generally, the term "sale or exchange" refers to a transfer of property to another party in exchange for monetary or other consideration. Even though the term "sale or exchange" is widely used in the Code, Regulations, official tax rulings and case law, there is no specific statutory definition of the phrase. Rather, the phrase "sale or exchange" or the term "sale" or "exchange" must be interpreted using its common meaning for tax purposes (as applied in the context of opportunity zones). While §1001(a) (determination of capital gains) uses the phrase "sale or other disposition," the phrase "sale or exchange" has a narrower meaning than a "sale or other disposition."[55] As a result, a transaction can be a "sale or other disposition" but still not be a "sale or exchange" of a capital asset. In addition, Congress has enacted a number of special provisions that determine whether or not certain transactions are treated as sales or exchanges.

The Tax Court has listed various factors indicating whether a sale or exchange exists: (1) whether legal title has passed; (2) how the parties treat the transaction; (3) whether the purchaser has acquired an equity interest in the property; (4) whether the transaction creates a current obligation on the seller to transfer legal title for an agreed-upon consideration; (5) whether the right to possession has vested in the purchaser; (6) which party pays the property taxes; (7) whether the purchaser bears the risk of loss; and (8) whether the purchaser receives the profits (including appreciation in the value of the property) from the operation and sale of the property.[56]

Although the term "sale" is not defined in the Code or in the Regulations, courts have generally used the ordinary meaning of the term (in common usage).[57] Thus, a sale has occurred when there is a transfer of property for money or its equivalent[58] or a promise to pay money.[59] Whether a sale has occurred, or whether an agreement is merely an intent to sell in the future, is typically an issue of fact.[60] The determination of whether a sale has occurred is governed by the tax law (and not necessarily by the taxpayer's intent), usually relying on applicable state law.[61]

An "exchange" is a transfer of property for other property.[62] The Supreme Court[63] interpreted Reg. §1.1001-1(a) to mean that properties that are exchanged must be materially different so as to embody "legally distinct entitlements." The Supreme Court has held that an exchange will be deemed to have occurred if the transferred assets are materially different, whether or not the parties have experienced a change in their economic positions.

One of the most common forms of a taxable exchange results from the material modification of a debt instrument.[64] In some circumstances, a taxpayer attempt to structure a debt workout to have it treated as a material modification (resulting in capital gains) instead of cancellation of indebtedness under §108.[65] Such a material modification would also be eligible for deferral under §1400Z-2(a)(1) as an "exchange" that resulted in capital gains.

## HOW ARE THE RELATED PARTY RULES APPLIED?

Section 1400Z-2(a)(1) only permits deferral of capital gains derived from the sale to, or exchange with, an "unrelated person". The Regulations further clarify that a capital gain from a sale or exchange with a person that is related to either (1) the eligible taxpayer that would recognize the gain if §1400Z-2(a)(1) or (2) any pass-through entity or other person recognizing and allocating the gain to the eligible taxpayer is not eligible for deferral.[66] For purposes of the QOZ program, persons are related under the tests of §267(b) and §707(b)(1), determined by substituting 20 percent for 50 percent (which has the effect of requiring transactions to be between taxpayers that are 80 percent unrelated).[67]

Section 267 is a common related party test used for many purposes of the Code. In general, under §267,the following persons are considered related for the purposes of §1400Z-2: (1) members of a family; (2) individual and a 20% owned corporation; (3) two corporations that are members of the same control group; (4) a grantor and a fiduciary of any trust; (5) a fiduciary of a trust and a fiduciary of another trust, if the same person is a grantor of both trusts; (6) a fiduciary of a trust and beneficiary of such trust; (7) a fiduciary of a trust and the beneficiary of another trust, if the same person is a grantor of both trusts; (8) a fiduciary of a trust and a corporation that is 20% owned by the grantor of such trust; (9) a person and a tax-exempt organization that is controlled by members of the family of such individual; (10) a corporation and partnership if the same person owns 20% or more of each entity; (11) an S corporation and another S corporation if the same persons own 20% of each; (12) an S corporation and a C corporation if the same person owns 20% or more of each entity; and (13) an executor of an estate and a beneficiary of such estate.[68]

Under §267, constructive ownership rules apply to determine whether an individual is deemed to own property that is indirectly owned by such individual or a close relative.[69] Under these rules, an individual is considered to own interests held by such individual's family. The family of an individual includes such individual's brothers and sisters, spouse, ancestor and lineal descendants.[70]

Section 707(b)(2) provides that that transactions between (A) partnership and a person owning (directly or indirectly) more than 20% of the capital interest, or the profits interest in such partnership or (B) 2 partnerships with the same person owning (directly or indirectly) more than 20% of the capital interests or profits interests, are subject to related party restrictions.

The effect of these related party rules is to define which relationships will be subject to the 80-percent related party tests. In large part, these rules capture most family relationships and affiliations between individuals and entities or trusts in which they or family members maintain ownership and/or control.

## HOW DOES A TAXPAYER MAKE AN ELECTION TO DEFER GAIN?

Section 1400Z-2(a)(1) provides that gain is deferred "at the election of the taxpayer". The IRS has issued instructions under its authority pursuant to which a taxpayer may defer gains.[71] On the taxpayer's income tax return, the taxpayer may defer the reinvested capital gains for in the manner as provided on page 10 of the Instructions to Form 8949. Specifically, the gain will be reported on Schedule D and Form 8949. The deferral will be reported as follows (*the below instructions are copied verbatim from the IRS Instructions for Form 8949*):

1.  Report the deferral of the eligible gain on its own row of Form 8949 in Part I with box C checked or Part II with box F checked (depending on whether the gain being deferred is short-term or long-term).

2.  If you made multiple investments in different QOFs or in the same QOF on different dates, use a separate row for each investment.

3.  If you invested eligible gains of the same character (but from different transactions) on the same date into the same QOF, you can group those investments on the same row.

4.  In column (a), enter only the EIN of the QOF into which you invested.

5.  In column (b), enter the date you invested in the QOF. Leave columns (c), (d), and (e) blank.

6.  Enter code "Z" in column (f) and the amount of the deferred gain as a negative number (in parentheses) in column (g).

If the taxpayer is deferring a §1231 gain, the deferral election will be made on Form 4797, Sales of Business Assets. In addition, the taxpayer must report the following:

"Each QOF investment of IRC section 1231 gains will use two separate rows in Part I (short-term transactions) or Part II (long-term transactions), as applicable, of Form 8949. For the second row, in column (a), enter only the EIN of the QOF investment. In column (b), enter the date of the QOF investment. Leave columns (c), (d), and (e) blank. Enter code "Z" in column (f) and the amount of the deferred gain as a negative number (in parentheses) in column (g)."

Additionally, the taxpayer will file Form 8997, Initial and Annual Statement of Qualified Opportunity Fund ("QOF") Investments. Form 8997 requires an investor to disclose all of its QOF investments held at the beginning and end of the tax year. Additionally, on the form, the investor will disclose any capital gains deferred by investing in a QOF and QOF investments disposed of during the current year.[72]

A failure to file Form 8997 for any taxable year will result in a rebuttable presumption that the taxpayer had has inclusion event (described in §1.1400Z2(b)-1(c) during the year).[73] The taxpayer may rebut the presumption by filing the required form or establishing to the satisfaction of the Commissioner that an inclusion event did not occur.

## WHEN DOES A PERSON OR ENTITY CONSTITUTE A 'TAXPAYER' ELIGIBLE TO MAKE AN ELECTION?

An eligible taxpayer is a person that is required to report the recognition of gains during the taxable year under federal income tax accounting principles, including individuals, C corporations (including RICs and REITs), partnerships, S corporations, trusts and estates.[74]

The statute, however, defines the investment in the QOF by reference to the taxpayer investing in the QOF (*i.e.*, in the case of gain from the sale of any property *by the taxpayer* . . . gross income shall not include the amount *invested by the taxpayer*). Thus, the taxpayer that is deferring the gain (whether the entity or individual owner) would be the investor if a look through rule does not apply.

However, the Regulations define a "QOF Partner" to mean a person that owns a qualifying interest directly or a person that "owns such qualifying investment through equity interests solely in one or more partnerships".[75] Thus, the Regulations contemplate individuals owning QOF interests through partnerships, even if this concept is not addressed explicitly.

## What Constitutes an "Investment"?

### Definition of an Investment

Under §1400Z-2(a)(1)(A), the deferred gains must be "invested by the taxpayer in a qualified opportunity fund" to be eligible for the respective tax benefits. What is an investment in a QOF? Investment can be in the form of cash or property, may be actual contributions or deemed contributions, and can be in the form of debt or equity.

The Regulations use the concept of an "eligible interest" to define what constitutes an eligible investment for purposes of the statute. An eligible interest is an equity interest in a QOF, including preferred stock or a partnership interest with special allocations.[76] Since an equity interest is required, the term eligible interest excludes any debt instrument within the meaning of §1275(a)(1) and §1.1275-1(d). Moreover, an eligible interest will retain that classification even if it is used as collateral for a loan, or in comparable situations.[77]

A taxpayer may use an eligible gain to purchase an eligible interest in a QOF from another person in a secondary transaction (and not directly from the issuer).[78] An eligible interest includes an interest in an eligible entity issued before the entity becomes a QOF. The Regulations do not restrict a taxpayer from acquiring an interest from a related person. This would permit a taxpayer, who may not have had sufficient capital gains at the time of the necessary investment, to buy an interest from a related person at a later date.

The Regulations also permit an interest in a QOF acquired from a person other than a QOF (that otherwise is treated as an eligible interest) to be treated as an eligible interest.[79] Accordingly, the acquisition of an eligible interest from an existing equity owner of a QOF will be a qualifying interest, however, the 10-year holding period will begin as of the date of acquisition by the new owner.

Although the statute is ambiguous regarding whether the investment in a QOF must be in the form of cash, the Regulations explicitly allow an investment to be made with cash or property.[80] Thus, a taxpayer makes an investment for purposes of §1400Z-2 if it transfers cash or property to a QOF in exchange for eligible interests in the QOF.[81]

Moreover, the use of debt may be used as an alternative to equity if an investor does not have any remaining capital gains. The Regulations describe how the contribution of property to a QOF is permitted. A QOF could issue a promissory note to an investor in exchange for cash. The taxpayer's subsequent contribution of the promissory note to the QOF in exchange for an interest (at a time that the investor has eligible capital gains) should be considered a qualifying investment with the value of the investment equal to the adjusted basis of the note (*i.e.*, the cash paid plus any recognized and unpaid interest).

*Comment*: There does not appear to be a restriction on the use of convertible debt. Arguably, a fund could structure its investment as a convertible note which is convertible at the initial fair market value and returns a coupon that is equivalent to the preferred return. The investor could then convert its debt into equity at any time which would allow the investor to control the timing of the investment of gains. Note, however, that the 10-year holding period would not begin until the time that such conversion was made and the economic rights of the equity holders and debt holders may differ (at least in regard to residual allocations of profits and/or cash flows).

Importantly, the Regulations provide that deemed contributions under §752(a) (relating to the tax treatment of the assumption of liabilities of a partner in a partnership being treated as contributing cash to such partnership under §752(a)) will <u>not</u> constitute an eligible investment (and the basis increase resulting from a §752 assumption of liabilities is disregarded in determining the portion of a partner's investment that is qualified).[82] This is consistent with the treatment of §752 liabilities for purposes the QOZ program (which also does not include §752 gain as eligible gain for reinvestment in the same QOF). Moreover, this treatment is fortunate for taxpayers that would otherwise have to determine if the assumption of a §752 liability would be treated as a contribution to the QOF, which would cause a mixed funds investment for such investor.

The amount of an investment that is treated as an eligible interest is limited to a taxpayer's elected deferred capital gains that it invests in the respective QOF.[83] If a taxpayer invests more than the amount of gain deferred, the excess will not be eligible for the opportunity zone tax benefits. Rather, such gains will be treated in the manner of mixed-investment funds.[84]

*Practice Tip*: Since debt is not considered an interest, a taxpayer may avoid having a mixed-fund investment by contributing cash for equity (in an amount up to the taxpayer's aggregate capital gains that may be deferred) and contributing any excess as debt (which may later be contributed).[85]

### Amount of an Investment

The amount of the investment in a QOF is equal to the amount of cash invested if the investment is made in cash.[86] In the case of a contribution of property (with adjusted basis different than such property's fair market value), the amount of the investment is based on the following rules:

1.  If the QOF's basis of the transferred property is determined by reference to the adjusted basis of the transferred property, the amount of the investment is equal to the lesser of the adjusted basis of the contributed property or the fair market value of the contributed property.[87]

2.  A potential trap exists for property owners that intend to contribute property to a QOF if a taxpayer contributes property with a fair market value that exceeds the taxpayer's adjusted basis. Such taxpayer will be deemed to have made an investment with mixed funds as described in §1400Z-2(e)(1).[88]  Thus, a portion of such investment will not qualify for opportunity zone tax benefits.

3.  The Regulations provide that in the case of property transferred with a built-in loss and §362(e)(2) applies (relating to determination of basis of property transferred to a corporation with a built in loss), the taxpayer is deemed to have made an election under §362(e)(2)(C) (limiting the basis of the transferee to the transferor's stock basis).[89]

4.  To the extent that a taxpayer contributes property to a QOF and the basis of the property is not determined by reference to the adjusted basis of the contributed property (such as in the case of property that causes gain recognition under §752), the amount of the investment will equal to the fair market value of the property immediately before the transfer.[90]

The effect of these rules is that when a taxpayer contributes property (other than cash) to a QOF, if the property value exceeds its adjusted basis (which is likely to be the case in the context of many development projects, particularly real estate developments), the taxpayer will be treated as having made an investment with mixed funds. A taxpayer could avoid having a mixed-funds investment with respect to the contribution of appreciated property to a QOF by instead *selling* property to the QOF (in exchange for cash or a note) and reinvesting any recognized gains (in another QOF).[91] However, the reinvestment of gains from such a sale is not available if such sale is considered made to a related party.[92]

A sale of appreciated property will have the effect of accelerating the seller's capital gain (since there are no gains resulting from a contribution of property). If the gains are reinvested, the acceleration will be delayed until the date that gain is included (usually December 31, 2026). The benefit is that the entire investment will be eligible for the QOZ tax benefits. If such a scenario arises, the investor should "run the numbers" to determine the best approach.

To the extent that an investment in a QOF consists of an eligible investment in part, and an investment that is not eligible, in part, it will be considered an investment with mixed funds. Under §1400Z-2(e)(1), such an investment will be treated as 2 separate investments: (i) an investment that was made with a qualifying investment and is subject to the rules for an eligible interest for which a deferral election was made and (ii) an investment for which no such election was made (which is not subject to the benefits under the QOZ program).[93]

### Special Rules for Partnerships

The Regulations also enacted specific rules regarding what will constitute an investment in a partnership.

1.      To qualify as an investment in a partnership, such investment must be treated as a contribution for tax purposes (*e.g.*, a transfer of property that is treated as a disguised sale is not considered an investment under §1400Z-2(a)(1)(A)).[94]

2.      If a contribution to a partnership is followed by a distribution of property that would be recharacterized as a disguised sale under §707 in certain circumstances relating to contribution of non-cash property or resulting from debt financed distributions, it will not be treated as an investment for purposes of §1400Z-2(a).[95]   For this purpose, any cash contributed is treated as non-cash property and in the case of a debt financed distribution to which Reg. §1.707-5(b) applies, the partner's share of liabilities is deemed to be zero.  **The effect of this rule is that a debt financed distribution within the first two years following the related contribution is almost always taxable.**[96]

3.      The Regulations provide rules that take into account debt basis and mixed fund investments to reflect that the amount of the taxpayer's investment is the lesser of the taxpayer's "net basis" or "net value" (to ensure consistent application with the basis rules applicable to mixed fund investments generally).

The Regulations also provide that an interest in a QOF may be acquired directly from a person other than the QOF (*i.e.*, an existing owner of such QOF interest).[97]  If a QOF is acquired from a person other than a QOF, the amount of the investment will equal the cash, or fair market value of other property, that the taxpayer exchanged for such QOF interest.  Note, however, that the purchaser must acquire such interest with reinvested capital gains in order for the investment to be treated as a qualifying investment.

Profits interests (*e.g.*, carried interests or promote interests) that are issued by a QOF to a taxpayer in exchange for services rendered or to be rendered are not considered an eligible investment since the interests were not issued in exchange for cash or property.[98] Query whether a different approach could be used in lieu of profits interests such that the speculative remaining value of a leveraged partnership could be acquired for cash (with the interest designed and valued in a similar manner as the risky tranches of a bond fund or CDO), resulting in such interest being treated as a qualifying interest rather than a profits interests issued in exchange for services.

The treatment of profits interests as nonqualified interests applies solely for the issuance of such interests by a QOF. There is no explicit prohibition against an upper-tier profits interest being issued by an entity that is a qualified investor in a QOF, with a fully qualifying investment in a QOF. Thus, if a partnership invests in a QOF, and issues a profits interest to a partner at the upper-tier level, the interests held by the partnership/investor that are qualified interests made with qualified gains will be fully qualified investments and the profits interests issued by the upper-tier entity may ultimately benefit from tax-free gains.[99]

## HOW IS THE 180-DAY PERIOD DETERMINED?

The 180-day rule provides that the 180-day period to reinvest capital gains begins on the date of the sale or exchange.[100] As the QOZ program became law, the question of when gain is recognized in various situations under the program was of paramount importance (as it drives the threshold requirement that the investment occur in the 180-day time period following the gain). The Regulations expand on this definition, providing that the 180-day period begins on the date that the gain would be recognized for federal income tax purposes (assuming the elections discussed below are not made). For example, the 180-day period begins on the trade date for a regular stock trade.[101]

The Regulations also provide an additional example that explicitly provides that the date that capital gains would be included from the disposition of an investment in a QOF begins the 180-day period to defer reinvestment of the now included gain (and a reinvestment in the same QOF is permitted).[102]

## RIC and REIT Capital Gains Dividends

When shareholder receives a capital gain dividend from a regulated investment company (RIC) or a real estate investment trust (REIT), the 180-day period generally begins on the last day of the shareholder's taxable year in which the capital gain would be recognized by the shareholder.[103] However, the shareholder of a RIC or REIT has the option to elect to treat the 180-day period as beginning on the date of the dividend distribution.[104] If the election is made, the aggregate amount of the eligible gain with respect to the aforementioned dividends is limited to the aggregate amount of capital gain dividends reported for that shareholder by the RIC or designated for that shareholder by the REIT for that shareholder's taxable year.[105] For example, when a REIT issues a capital gain dividend on March 1, the shareholder has the option to begin the 180-day period on December 31 or, if an election is made, March 1, as long as the aggregate deferral of dividends from that REIT do not exceed the aggregate capital gain dividends from REIT for the taxable year.[106] If multiple dividends are issued by the RIC or REIT on different dates during a taxable year, the shareholder can determine the 180-day period for each dividend, without consideration for the other.[107]

When there are undistributed capital gains that are required to be included as long-term capital gains, pursuant to §852(b)(3)(D) or §857(b)(3)(C), the shareholder can elect whether the 180-day period begins on the last day of the RIC's or REIT's taxable year or the last day of the shareholder's taxable year.[108]

### Partnerships, S-Corporation and Other Passthrough Entities

Importantly, the Regulations created substantial flexibility for taxpayers by permitting elective provisions that favor either partnerships or their partners (or similar pass-through entities). These rules (detailed below) are complicated. However, the following steps reflect how partnership gains are treated by the respective partnerships and their partners:

1. The partnership (other than a partnership that is also a QOF) that recognizes gain determines whether it will defer some or all of such gain by making an investment in a QOF.[109]

2. Any gain not deferred by such partnership is included in its partners' distributive share.

3. Each partner that elects to defer gain included in its distributive share will either use as its recognition date to start the 180 day clock (1) the last day of the partnership's tax year; (2) unextended due date of the partnership's tax return; or (3) elect to use the date that the partnership recognized the gain to start the 180-day time period.

A partnership is an eligible taxpayer and may elect to defer recognition of income (at the partnership level) under §1400Z-2(a).[110]  If a partnership makes such an election to defer gain, the deferred gain is deferred under the rules of §1400Z-2, and the deferred gain is not included in the partners' distributive shares (and such amounts are included in the partner's shares if the partnership does not defer gain recognition).[111]

When a partner's distributive shares include eligible gains with respect to the partner, the partner may elect to defer some or all of the eligible gain under §1400Z-2(a)(1)(A) and the Regulations.[112] When a partner has an opportunity to make the deferral, 180-day period will generally begin on the last day of the partnership's tax year (or such partner's last day in which its allocable share includes such eligible gain).[113] Alternatively, the partner may instead elect that 180-day period begin on either (1) same date that would have been the underlying partnership's commencement of the 180-day period; or (2) beginning on the due date for the partnership's tax return without extension, for the taxable year in which the gain was realized.[114] The final Regulations provide excellent flexibility when a partner is provided an opportunity to reinvest eligible gains. For example, if a partnership elects not to defer a capital gain that occurred in March 1, 2019, the partner's 180-day period could begin on December 31, 2019 or, if an election is made, on March 1 2019 or March 15, 2020.

When §1231 or §1256 gain is involved, the default rule is that the gain is recognized on the last day of the tax year. However, if the partnership does not elect to defer the gain, the partner would be able to use the last day of the tax year or due date of the partnership's tax return, without extension to calculate the beginning of its 180-day period reinvestment period.

Rules similar to those applicable for partnerships also apply in the case of S corporation, trusts and estates.[115] In a situation when a grantor trust realizes the gain, either the trust or owner can make the deferral election, regardless of whether the gain was distributed to the deemed owner of the trust.[116]

*Practice Tip:* Many taxpayers would benefit (and create additional flexibility) by transferring securities or closely held stock to a partnership which could enable such taxpayers to increase the time period eligible for deferral to over 21 months in some cases.

For the purposes of the respective provisions that provide for gain recognition as of the last day of the tax year, or on December 31, 2026, the first day of the 180-day period is December 31 or the last day of the tax year (and not the first day of the subsequent tax year). Thus, if the last day of the tax year is December 31, 2026 with respect to any eligible gain, the last day for possible reinvestment will be June 28, 2027.

While the Code and Regulations do not provide relief for failing to reinvest timely, the IRS found grounds for relief when a Taxpayer failed to invest within the 180-day investment period for a shareholder in an S-corporation that received incorrect advice from an attorney.[117]

## ABILITY OF A QOF TO REINVEST ITS GAINS

Section 1400Z-2(e)(4) generally provides authority for the Secretary to issue Regulations allowing a QOF a reasonable amount of time to reinvest the return of capital (i.e., the original investment of deferred gains). Under the Regulations, a QOF is granted twelve months to reinvest proceeds from the return of capital or the sale or disposition of some or all of its QOZP.[118] This time period may be extended up to twelve months if investment is delayed due to a Federally declared disaster.[119]

During the time period in which such proceeds are held by the QOF, such assets are treated as QOZP for purposes of the 90-percent investment standard so long as they are held in cash, cash equivalents or debt instruments with a term of 18 months or less.[120]

*Practice Note*: When a QOF disposes of property that generates a new gain and results in an inclusion event for the original deferred gain, the QOF will treat these separate components differently. The gain that represents return of capital to the QOF (*i.e.*, the original invested capital that was deferred at the time of the investment) is eligible to be reinvested by the QOF within twelve months. The new gain is eligible for reinvestment in a QOF (but a QOF may not make an investment in a another QOF). Practically, the QOF will need to distribute the new gains to its shareholders who would reinvest that amount in a QOF since any such reinvestment must otherwise meet the requirements for gains to be reinvested under §1400Z-2(a).

# CHAPTER SEVEN

# Deferral and Inclusion of Capital Gains

Section 1400Z-2(b) describes the timing of deferred gains and when such gains are included in income. Gain that is properly deferred under §1400Z-2(a) will be included in income on the earlier of (i) the date that such investment is sold or exchanged; or (ii) December 31, 2026.[121] The result of this rule is that the deferred gain (or the fair market value of the investment, if less) will be recognized on December 31, 2026, with the tax liability generally due on April 15, 2027 (subject to estimated tax penalties, if applicable).

If the investor holds the investment for sufficient time before the date that gain is included in income (generally December 31, 2026), the amount of the gain will be reduced. The original gain that is included is reduced by ten-percent if the investment is held for 5 years and the amount of the gain that is included in income is reduced by another five-percent if the investment in the QOF is held for at least 7 years (in each cases, the holding period must be met prior to the date that gain is included in income to obtain the gain reduction).

## EVENTS CAUSING INCLUSION OF GAIN IN INCOME (OR NOT)

The reinvested gain is deferred until December 31, 2026 unless the taxpayer is considered to have sold or exchanged its interest at an earlier date.  In some cases, the determination of whether an investment has been sold or exchanged is straightforward (as in the case of an actual sale of an interest to a third party for cash).  In other cases, however, a taxpayer is deemed to have sold or exchanged all, or part, of its investment and is therefore required to include deferred gain into income.

*Planning Tip:* A gain recognized upon an inclusion event that occurs prior to December 31, 2026 can be further deferred through an investment in QOF, so long as all other requirements of §1400Z-2 are met.

 The Regulations detail the circumstances in which previously deferred gain is included in income and will be taxed (referred to as an "inclusion event").  Thus, the Regulations provide the general rule that deferred gain is included in gross income on the earlier of the (1) date of an inclusion event or (2) December 31, 2026.[122]

**The Regulations provide a list of the transactions that are considered inclusion events.[123]  The determination of what constitutes an inclusion event is one of the most technical and complicated areas of the regulatory regime.**

The determination of gain inclusion is subject to special rules and not based solely on general income tax principles since the investment in a QOF is effectively made with pre-tax dollars (until inclusion). While the return of cash or property in a traditional investment vehicle may be properly considered the return of capital that reduces a taxpayer's basis in its investment, an investor in a QOF has no basis with respect its investment (except for debt basis after two years) and certain transactions must then be characterized as the inclusion of previously deferred gain.[124] **Any transaction involving a QOF interest (e.g., transfer, distribution) could lead to the inadvertent inclusion of gains under the QOZ program (prior to December 31, 2026) even if the same transaction would not be taxable under general income tax principles.**

## GENERAL RULES FOR INCOME INCLUSION

The first inclusion rule (and the general rule) provides that if, and to the extent that, such event (i) causes a reduction of a taxpayer's equity interest in a QOF; (ii) is a distribution of property (other than cash) regardless of whether the taxpayer's direct interest in the QOF is reduced; (iii) results in the taxpayer claiming a loss for worthlessness with respect to its qualifying investment in a QOF, or (iv) causes a QOF to loses its status as a QOF,[125] such event will be an inclusion event (except as otherwise provided below).

The equity reduction rule and worthless equity rule were sensible in light of the statutory language causing inclusion as of the date of a sale or exchange. However, the treatment of any property distribution as an inclusion event effectively functions as a mechanism to prevent potentially abusive property transfers to equity holders that had previously deferred gains on the disposition of property, and also effectively causes any distribution within two years to be treated as a taxable inclusion event.

## Terminations and Liquidations

The termination of a QOF (for federal income tax purposes) is considered an inclusion event.[126] If the QOF ceases to exist for federal income tax purposes, the taxpayer has an inclusion event with respect to all of its qualifying investment. This rule applies whether or not the liquidation of the QOF would otherwise be treated as a gain recognition event. Thus, in the case of a partnership termination followed by an in-kind distribution of the partnership's assets to its partners (which would otherwise be generally non-taxable under §731 and §736), this rule would cause gain inclusion for purposes of §1400Z-2(b). For example, if a QOF, taxed as a partnership, converts to a QOF C corporation (or vice versa) the conversion is an inclusion event for all QOF owners with respect to their entire qualifying investment.[127] Investors and their advisors should be very cautious with respect to QOF restructuring during the deferral period to avoid the consequences of this rule.

The liquidation of an *owner* of a QOF is also treated as an inclusion event in certain circumstances.[128] Specifically, a distribution of a qualifying investment in complete liquidation of a QOF owner is an inclusion event to the extent that §336(a) treats the distribution as if the qualifying investment were sold to the distributee at its fair market value (without regard to §336(d) (relating to the limitation of losses for certain corporate liquidations)).[129] However, a distribution of a qualifying investment to a distributee in a corporate liquidation will not be considered an inclusion event to the extent that §337(a) applies to the transaction (nonrecognition treatment in the case of a distribution to an 80-percent shareholder in a complete liquidation).[130] The QOF owner's holding period (that is subject to a §337(a) transaction) tacks pursuant to §1223(1) or (4).[131]

### *Lifetime Gifts and Transfers Upon Death*

The Regulations contain fairly detailed rules regarding gifts and transfers at death that result in limitations on potential gifting of investments that hold QOF interests and provide for reasonable flexibility for QOF investments held at death.

## Gifts

Most transfers by gift are also considered inclusion events. A transfer of a qualifying investment by gift, whether outright or in trust, is an inclusion event (this results applies even if the transfer is not considered a completed gift for Federal gift tax purposes, and regardless of the taxable or tax exempt status of the donee).[132]

This rule has one important exception: if the owner of a qualifying investment contributes it to a grantor trust (such that under the grantor trust rules, the transferor is the deemed owner of the trust), such contribution is not an inclusion event.[133]  The contribution of an investment to a grantor trust will often be treated as a gift for gift tax purposes, but will not be treated as a contribution, sale or exchange for income tax purposes (such transactions are often referred to as transfers to a "defective grantor trust" which is recognized as a separate trust for gift and estate tax purposes).

The preamble to the Proposed Regulations explicitly provides that a transfer by gift to a grantor trust is not an inclusion event. Indeed, the preamble states (in §VII, Part E) that "[t]he rationale for this exception is that, for Federal income tax purposes, the owner of the grantor trust is treated as the owner of the property in the trust until such time that the owner releases certain powers that cause the trust to be treated as a non-grantor trust. Accordingly, the owner's qualifying investment is not reduced or eliminated for Federal income tax purposes upon the transfer to such a grantor trust."

The grantor trust exception applies in the case of a contribution to a grantor trust. For estate planning purposes, assets are often sold to a 'defective' grantor trust in exchange for a cash down payment and a promissory note for the balance (in a transaction that is not recognized for income tax purposes).[134] In such a circumstance, the transfer is generally ignored for income tax purposes (even though it is, economically, a sale or exchange). Since a sale to a grantor trust is ignored for income tax recognition purposes, given the underlying rationale of not treating a transfer to a grantor trust as an inclusion event, a sale to a defective grantor trust should also be permitted without causing gain inclusion.

## Estates

Generally, transfers that occur solely as a result of the death of a taxpayer and the administration of such taxpayer's estate to do not result in gain inclusion.[135] Thus, the following transactions are not considered inclusion events: (i) a transfer to a decedent's estate as a result of the owner's death; (ii) a distribution of a qualifying investment by the deceased owner's estate; (iii) a distribution of a qualifying investment by a deceased owner's trust that is made by reason of the deceased owner's death; (iv) the passing of jointly owned qualifying property to the surviving co-owner by operation of law; or (v) any other transfer of a qualifying investment at death by operation of law.

On the other hand, dispositions involving estates that are not considered to have been made as a result of the owner's death will be inclusions events.[136] Such transactions (to the extent not explicitly permissible as described above) include (i) a sale, exchange or other disposition by the deceased taxpayer's estate or trust; (ii) any disposition by a legatee, heir or beneficiary of the deceased owner's estate who received the qualifying investment as a result of the taxpayer's death; and (iii) any disposition by the surviving joint owner or other recipient that received the interest as a result of the taxpayer's death.

Presumably, the rules described above will not cause gain inclusion if such interest is transferred first to a beneficiary as a result of the original owner's death, and then transferred as a result of the second owner's death. Since the beneficiary receives such property without causing an inclusion event since it was received in a distribution as a result of the original owner's death, such person becomes the owner of the investment. In such capacity, the above rules should prevent the inclusion resulting from an otherwise permissible transfer at the second owner's death. This result is important for older investors that may not live to until the QOF interest is sold and intend to leave their assets to a surviving spouse, and then to their descendants.

To the extent that a qualifying interest in a QOF is owned by a grantor trust, the change to non-grantor trust status (other than by reason of the grantor's death) will be an inclusion event.[137] Likewise, the creation of grantor trust status (by a non-grantor trust) is an inclusion event. These grantor trust rules are otherwise subject to the inclusion rules of Reg. §1.1400Z2(b)-1(c)(4) (relating to the distributions and dispositions upon the death of an owner).

**Importantly, if held by a defective grantor trust, a QOF interest can effectively achieve an after-death basis step up for an asset that is otherwise not included in a decedent's estate.** Most practitioners take the position that an asset is not included in a decedent's estate if it was transferred to a grantor trust that is not included in the decedent's estate under §2038, the estate (or trust) is not entitled to a basis step up under

§1014. However, a tax-free step up could be achieved under the QOZ program as described below.

Assume that a taxpayer transfers an interest in a QOF (by gift) to a defective grantor trust and subsequently dies while the defective grantor trust holds the investment. Under the rules applicable to grantor trusts and QOF interests, the death of a grantor will cause the trust to be treated as a non-grantor trust. However, the conversion to non-grantor trust status as a result of the grantor's death is not an inclusion event.[138] Following the death of a grantor during the ten year holding period, the QOF interest will be held by the trust (which has converted to a non-grantor trust). Following the sale or exchange of the QOF interest (or the underlying assets), the effect is that the trust receives a basis step up under §1400Z-2(c) and that the gain is tax-free to the trust. Thus, the taxpayer would have removed the QOF interests from its estate through the gift of the interest during lifetime, but the trust will receive a basis step up at disposition. The net effect is that the QOF interest will never be taxed for estate *or* income tax purposes under this fact pattern.[139]

### Partnership Non-Recognition Transactions

The Regulations provide for special rules in the case of a partnership that is a QOF, or that directly or indirectly own interests in a QOF, such that the inclusion rules apply to such partner's share of a QOF to the extent of its share of gain of that underlying QOF.[140] These rules are primarily intended to avoid causing inclusion in the case of certain partnership non-recognition transactions.

First, the contribution of a QOF owner (including a contribution by a partner or partnership that owns interests in a QOF solely through upper tier partnerships), of its direct or indirect interest in a qualifying investment (*a contributing partner*) to a partnership in a transaction that is tax-free under §721(a) (*a transferee partnership*) is not an inclusion event (except in the case that it results in a termination of the partnership QOF or the direct or indirect owner of a QOF under §708(b)(1)).[141] Importantly, when read literally, this section reflects that the termination of an upper-tier partnership that is an indirect owner of a qualifying interest in a QOF will be an inclusion event (even in a transaction for that will otherwise result in no recognition of gain or loss). A partnership transaction for which §721(a) does not apply will be subject to the inclusion rules otherwise applicable under Reg. §1.1400Z2(b)-1(c).

Second, a merger or consolidation of a partnership holding a qualifying investment (directly or indirectly through one or more partnerships) in a transaction for which §708(b)(2)(A) (relating to the treatment of a merged or consolidated partnership as a continuation of the preexisting partnerships) will not be an inclusion event.[142]

Following any permitted partnership transaction (as described in the preceding two paragraphs), the transferee partnership or surviving partnership must allocate and report the gain with respect to the qualifying investment to the same extent that the gain would have been allocated and reported (to the same partner or partners) in the absence of such contribution.[143]

### Partnership Distributions

Partnerships may generally make distributions to a partner on a tax-free basis, to the extent that the fair market value of the cash or other property that is distributed to a partner does not exceed the partner's basis (including debt basis) of its investment.[144] Often, leveraged partnerships make distributions from financing proceeds (*i.e.*, debt-financed distributions) without causing gain recognition since the distributee partner's share of liabilities (as determined under §752 and the Regulations promulgated thereunder) is greater than the value of the cash or property distributed. This rule is extended to leveraged QOZ partnerships explicitly, such that notwithstanding the general inclusion rule, actual or deemed distributions of property (including cash) to a partner by a partnership result in gain only if the fair market value of the distributed property exceeds the taxpayer's basis in its qualifying investment.[145]

Notwithstanding the general rule, most distributions within the first two years following a partner's contribution will be recharacterized as a disguised sale even if the same transaction would constitute a tax-free debt financed distribution under regular tax rules as a result of the special rules applicable to QOF contributions under the Regulations.[146] The effect of these rules is that all cash contributions are treated as non-cash property contributions, and the investor's share of partnership liabilities under §752 is equal to zero. The effect is that the investor will not have any basis for any debt-financed distribution for the first two years following any contribution.

### *Treatment of Mixed-Funds*

The partnership rules applicable to qualified opportunity zone investments also provide special rules in the case of mixed-use funds. In general, a taxpayer with mixed-funds investment (*i.e.*, a qualifying portion and a non-qualifying portion of an investment in a QOF partnership) will be treated, for purposes of §1400Z-2, as holding two separate interests in the QOF.[147] The separate interests rule is applicable for purposes of (i) determining basis (with the qualifying and non-qualifying investment having separate bases in the same manner as if they were held by separate taxpayers);[148] (ii) allocations and distributions under §704(b), and allocation of liabilities under §752 (which are both deemed made to the separate interests);[149] (iii) subsequent contributions (requiring a revaluation of separate interests and the adjustment of allocation percentages);[150] and (iv) allocation percentages, which shall be determined based on the relative capital contributions attributable to the qualifying and non-qualifying investment.[151]

**Profits Interests**

In the case of a partner that received a profits interest in exchange for services (which is a non-qualifying investment), the allocation percentages of such partner shall be calculated based on (i) with respect to the profits interest received, the highest share of residual profits the mixed-fund partner would receive with respect to such interest, and (ii) with respect to the remaining interest, the percentage interests for the capital interests (based on the relative values of qualifying and non-qualifying interests).[152] This has the effect of increasing the non-qualifying portion of the interest since the profits interest percentage will apply only using the maximum percentage of such profits interest (disregarding any allocation of residual profits for which there is not a reasonable likelihood of application). **There does not appear to be a prohibition on the use of a profits interest at an upper-tier partnership that itself has made an election for deferral (and will later make an election to step-up basis after 10 years) to avoid having such interests treated as a mixed-fund investment.**

Under this profits interest rule, an owner of a promote interest may have a greater share of its interest be treated as nonqualifying (based on the highest percentage rule) as compared to the actual economics of a sale or exchange. It may make sense to counter the negative ramifications of the above rule for the owner of a promote interest that also contributed capital by making the investment and issuing the profits (promote) interests to separate taxpayers (one holding a capital interest and one holding a profits interest) so that a disproportionate share of the gains will not be taxed (and gains will therefore be more closely aligned with the taxable and non-taxable portion of the interests).

## Remaining Gain Reduction Rule

Finally, the special partnership provisions provide that an inclusion event occurs when and to the extent that a transaction has the effect of reducing (i) the amount of remaining deferred gain of one or more of the direct or indirect partners, or (ii) the amount of gain that would be recognized by such partner(s) at the time of an inclusion event.[153]  This rule attempts to align the treatment of deferred gain with the amount of gain includible (and is referred to as the "remaining gain reduction rule").

It is unclear how the remaining gain reduction rule should be applied.  For example, a partner may be entitled to a cash flow preference such that it receives its invested capital plus a preferred return and is also entitled to a share of the residual interests.  The investor may receive cash flow from operations or through refinancing distributions that reduce the remaining preferred return.  Such transactions could, in theory, reduce the remaining deferred gain if the value of the investment falls below the amount of the remaining deferred gain.  The gain would be included "when and to what extent" the remaining deferred gain is reduced.  In most cases, this value cannot be ascertained with any degree of certainty since we do not know what the value will be on December 31, 2026 (and therefore do not know to what extent the remaining deferred gain is reduced, if at all).

For example, it is not unusual for equity value of preferred investors to be reduced due to a cash out refinance that returns capital to such investors.  The value may even be decreased substantially with a substantial portion of the invested equity returned to an investor through a cash out refinance.  However, the value of the residual equity will continue to increase as debt is repaid and property values increase, often resulting in no actual reduction in deferred gain as of December 31, 2026.

*Observation*: The remaining gain reduction rule could cause an inclusion event with a cash-out refinance (even after the two year period in which a debt-financed distribution would likely be characterized as a debt-financed distribution) if any portion of an investor's equity is returned (which is typical with leveraged real estate investments) such that the value of their remaining interest is less than the remaining deferred gain to the extent that such amount could be definitively determined.

## Tracking of Separate Interests

The separate interests rule (used by taxpayers to track mixed fund investments) creates some level of administrative and taxpayer complexity. In most circumstances, the respective partnership tracks important information relating to partnership tax items. However, in a QOF with mixed-fund investments, only the investor has knowledge of the investments and portions thereof attributable to qualified and non-qualified investments (subject to notification requirements described at the end of this Chapter). Accordingly, the taxpayer will bear the responsibility to make these determinations. This is not very much of a burden in the case of a single investment. However, taxpayers with multiple investments in a fund (or funds), as well as taxpayers that have an investment and also receive a profits interest, will endure greater complexity under the separate interests rule.

### *Rules Applicable to S Corporations*

The Regulations similarly apply special rules for S corporations that are either a QOF or an investor (directly or indirectly) in a QOF. Certain transactions specific to S corporations are explicitly not treated as inclusion events: (i) an election, revocation or termination of S corporation status under §1362;[154] (ii) a conversion of a qualified subchapter S trust (as defined in §1361(d)(3) (a "QSST")) to an electing small business trust (as defined in §1361(e)(1) ("an "ESBT");[155] (iii) a conversion of an ESBT to a QSST;[156] and (iv) a valid modification of a trust agreement by an S corporation shareholder.[157]

An actual or constructive distribution of property from a QOF S corporation to a shareholder with respect to its qualifying investment is an inclusion event only to the extent that the distribution is treated as gain from the sale or exchange of property under §1368(b)(2) and (c) (reflecting that distributions in excess of basis are treated as gain from the sale or exchange of property).[158] Unlike partners in partnerships, S corporation shareholders do not have basis from S corporation liabilities. As a result, debt-financed distributions will often result in gain for S corporation shareholders (which is an inclusion event) even if identical transactions in the partnership context would not result in current gain inclusion.

The Regulations also provide a spillover rule for S corporations such that adjustments to basis (that are generally applied pro rata to a shareholder's interests) are instead applied separately for qualifying investments and non-qualifying investments.[159] Effectively, the shareholder tracks its qualifying and non-qualifying interests separately, and basis adjustments are likewise applied separately.

The conversion of an S corporation to either a partnership or a disregarded entity is an inclusion event,[160] unless such conversion is treated as a qualifying §381 transaction.[161] To the extent an S corporation engages in a redemption that is treated as a distribution or property (to which §302(d) applies), such distribution will be treated as an inclusion event only to the extent that the distributions exceed the shareholder's basis in the QOF.[162]

The Regulations also clarify that differing rights of S corporation stock for a QOF or QOF equity owner will not be treated as separate classes of stock under §1361(b)(1).[163]   All of the provisions applicable to S corporations under Reg. §1.1400Z2(b)-1(c)(7) apply to such S corporation to the extent that it is a QOF, or the QOF shareholder.

### Rules Applicable to All Eligible Corporations (including C Corporations)

A distribution of property by a corporation with respect to a qualifying investment is not an inclusion event except to the extent that §301(c)(3) (relating to distributions in excess of basis being treated as a sale or exchange) applies to the distribution.[164]   Likewise, a redemption that is treated as a distribution of property (under §302(d)) is an inclusion amount for the full amount of the distribution.[165]   However, if all of the stock of a QOF is held by a single shareholder, or directly by members of a consolidated group, and if shares are redeemed in a redemption that is treated as a distribution of property, then the transaction will only be treated as an inclusion event to the extent that §301(c)(3) (relating to distributions in excess of basis being treated as a sale or exchange) applies to the distribution.[166]

The Regulations also provide specific rules for certain extraordinary corporate transactions as follows.

- §381 transactions (relating to certain corporate acquisitions, including asset acquisitions) will generally not be considered inclusion events if the acquirer is a QOF immediately after acquisition,[167] subject to inclusion rules in the case of boot distributed to shareholders.[168]

- §355 transactions (relating to distribution of stock of controlled corporations) are also subject to special rules: (i) distribution of stock by a QOF corporation is generally considered an inclusion event with respect to its qualifying investment;[169] and (ii) to the extent that a QOF distributes stock of a controlled corporation, and after such distribution both the distributing corporation and controlled corporations are QOFs immediately after the final distribution in a qualifying §355 transaction, the distribution will not be treated as an inclusion event.[170] Moreover, if a §355 transaction results in the reduction of a QOF shareholders' "direct tax ownership" of qualifying stock, the shareholder will have an inclusion event to the extent of such reduction.[171]

- Type "E" reorganizations (a recapitalization governed by §368(a)(1)(E)) and §1036 transactions (stock for stock transactions of the same corporation) will generally not be treated as inclusion events, except to the extent of boot distributed to shareholders, or of the shareholder's equity in QOF stock is reduced.[172]

- A §304 transaction (a redemption through the use of related corporations) will be treated as an inclusion event to the extent of the consideration received by the QOF shareholder.[173]

## Transfers Between Spouses (or Incident to Divorce)

A transfer between spouses or incident to divorce, or otherwise as provided in §1041, is an inclusion event.[174] Even though §1041 transactions are treated as nonrecognition events for federal income tax purposes, any such transfers are treated as a disposition of a qualifying investment in the QOF.

## Decertification

The decertification of a QOF, whether through a self-decertification or an involuntary decertification is an inclusion event.[175] The self-decertification can occur anytime and becomes effective at the beginning of the month following the month specified by the taxpayer (that cannot be earlier than the decertification filing).[176]

## HOLDING PERIOD

The holding period for a QOF investment is also clarified by the Regulations. The holding period for a qualifying investment is subject to the following rules: (i) the length of a time a qualifying investment has been held is determined without regard to the period which the taxpayer held property exchanged for such investment;[177] (ii) §1223(1) principles will apply in determining the holding period of stock acquired in a transaction for which §355, §368(a)(1)(E), §381 or §1036 will apply;[178] and (iii) a tacked holding period will be applicable to persons that received qualifying investments as a gift or by reason of the prior owner's death, which was not an inclusion event.[179] The effect of these rules is to reflect that QOF property acquired in a non-recognition event (*i.e.*, the QOF property was originally acquired with eligible gains, and is then transferred in a nonrecognition transaction) will receive a tacked holding period. This is the correct result as it follows the intent of the program. Likewise, no tacked holding period arises in the event of an exchange since that transaction is not considered a gain recognition event that preceded the QOF investment.

Consistent with the foregoing rules, QOF assets acquired in a §355 or §381 transaction will continue to be treated as qualified opportunity zone property, and the same principles also apply for purposes of determining whether the original use commences with such entity.[180] The Regulations also provide that the principles described in the previous sentence will also apply to partnership interests with regard to non-inclusion transactions.[181]

## AMOUNT OF GAIN INCLUDED IN INCOME FOR AN INCLUSION EVENT OR ON DECEMBER 31, 2026

In general, a taxpayer will recognize gain (with respect to the originally deferred gain) equal to the lesser of the (A) remaining deferred capital gains for the 2026 tax year; or (B) the fair market value of its equity investment (as of December 31, 2026), in each case reduced by any QOF basis adjustments. The QOF basis adjustment will either be 0%, 10% or 15% of the original deferred gain, depending on the taxpayer's holding period.

Specifically, the amount of gain that is included in gross income at the time of any inclusion event (or December 31, 2026) is the amount by which (i) the *lesser of* (A) the amount of gain excluded under the gain deferral rules of §1400Z-2(a)(1) or (B) the fair market value of the investment as of December 31, 2026 (or the date of inclusion, if different), exceeds (ii) the taxpayer's basis in the investment.[182] A taxpayer's basis in its investment for purposes of applying the inclusion rules under §1400Z-2 will be zero, except for adjustments with respect (i) gain inclusion of previously deferred gain or (ii) statutory basis adjustments under §§1400Z-2(b)(2)(B)(iii)-(iv).[183] Finally, the Regulations explicitly provide that the maximum gain that is included after the five-year and seven-year basis adjustments of §1400Z-2(b)(2)(B) is limited to the amount deferred under §1400Z-2(a)(1), less the amount of the basis adjustments allowed under §1400Z-2(b)(2)(B).

The Regulations provides additional detail on applying this rule in the context of partial inclusion events by adopting the following rule:

The amount of gain includible is equal to the excess of (*copied verbatim from the Regulations*):[184]

> (i) the lesser of (A) an amount which bears the same proportion to the remaining deferred gain, as (x) the fair market value of the

portion of the qualifying investment that is disposed of in the inclusion event (as determined on the date of the inclusion event), bears to (y) the fair market value of the total qualifying investment before the inclusion event, or (B) the fair market value of the portion of the qualifying investment that is disposed of in the inclusion event (as determined on the date of the inclusion event).

(ii) the fair market value of that portion (described in Reg. §1.1400Z2(b)-1(e)(1)(i)(A)(1)) is determined by multiplying the fair market value of taxpayer's qualifying investment in the QOF, valued on the date of the inclusion event, by the percentage of the taxpayer's qualifying investment that is represented by the portion disposed of in the inclusion event.

In many cases, the amount of gain that is includible upon the occurrence of an inclusion event is not easily determinable. As these rules provide, the lesser of rule requires taxpayers to determine the fair market value of their respective interests and will only include in income the lesser of such fair market value or the remaining deferred gain, reduced by the basis of such investment as determined under §1400Z-2.[185] By limiting the remaining deferred gain to the lesser of the (a) remaining deferred gain or (b) fair market value of the QOF interests as of December 31, 2026, the gain included is effectively reduced if the fair market value of the investment declines by December 31, 2026. However, these rules were modified for partnerships to avoid inadvertent benefits to partners not intended under the QOZ program (see the following section).

The inclusion rules provide a number of circumstances in which gain is recognized for property distributions; in these situations, the amount of gain included in income is the lesser of (i) the remaining deferred gain or (ii) the amount that gave rise to the inclusion event.[186]

The Regulations also issue clarifying rules which apply to gains that are deferred by S corporations or partnerships that are designed to apply the included deferred gain to the shareholders or partners (as the case may be), in proportion to their respective share of such deferred gain.[187]

## Special Rules for Partnerships

The Regulations contain a special rule for partnerships. Reg. §1.1400Z2(b)-1(e)(4) provides that, for inclusion events involving partnerships and S corporations, the amount includible is equal to the percentage of the qualifying QOF partnership or QOF S corporation interest disposed of, multiplied by the lesser of (1) the remaining deferred gain less the five-year and seven-year basis adjustments; or (2) the gain that would be recognized by the partner or shareholder if the interest were sold in a fully taxable transaction for its then fair market value.[188] Note that this approach under the Regulations is substantially different than that under the statute which merely says that the amount of gain included in income is the lesser of the deferred gain or the fair market value of the investment (with no reference to the amount taxable upon disposition).

Indeed, the changes from the statute do not follow the statutory language (but should be viewed as consistent with legislative intent). The commentary to the Regulations addresses this point:

> "Several commenters requested that the special amount includible rule for partnerships and S corporations be changed to follow the statutory language in section 1400Z-2(b)(2)(A). Commenters acknowledged that the special amount includible rule was intended to prevent taxpayers from avoiding the recognition of deferred gain upon an inclusion event when the fair market value of their qualifying investment has diminished due to debt-financed deductions or distributions. However, these

commenters emphasized that the special amount includible rule creates inequitable results for debt-financed losses attributable to periods before December 31, 2026, as compared to debt-financed losses incurred after this date. Certain commenters also suggested that this rule has adversely affected the ability to develop low-income housing tax credit projects and other community development properties in QOZs."[189]

Nevertheless, the Regulations adopted the rule requiring the gain inclusion to be based on the gain if such investment was sold in a fully taxable transaction at fair market value.

The Regulations also have a special rule for basis of partnerships. The initial basis is zero, as adjusted by the contributing partner's share of liabilities under §752.[190] Any basis adjustment under §1400Z-2(b)(2)(B)(iii)-(iv) is basis for all purposes.

The effect of this rule is to potentially increase the taxable gain at disposition as a result of prior losses and distributions, but not in excess of the remaining deferred gain.

At the time of the inclusion event, the taxpayer will recognize gain equal to the lesser of the (A) remaining deferred gain, less any basis adjustments under the 5-year rule and 7-year rule, or (B) the gain that would be recognized in a fully taxable transaction if the interest were sold in a fully taxable transaction for fair market value (determined as of December 31, 2026). In determining the actual tax consequences of these transactions, the following tax issues may be implicated: (1) the relationship between losses from a partnership and the gain recognized at an inclusion event; (2) determination of fair market value of the investment as of December 31, 2026 under federal tax principles; (3) strategic planning for depreciation in the QOZ context.

## Implications of the "Lesser Of" Rule

The effect of allowing taxpayers to include only the lesser of the gain or the fair market value is particularly significant in two respects: valuation issues and economic benefit of a reduced gain inclusion

First, the taxpayer must determine the fair market value of its investment as of any inclusion date or on December 31, 2026. In general, the valuation of the investment will follow the general valuation principles commonly utilized to value closely held interests.[191] The general rule articulated under prior tax rulings is to define fair market value as the "price at which the property would change hands between a willing buyer and a willing seller, neither being under any compulsion to buy or sell and both having reasonable knowledge of relevant facts." In this context, an appraiser will almost always apply discounts for lack of control and lack of marketability of QOF interests (which will almost always be closely held business interests).

The "lesser of" rule creates administrative complexity and lack of clarity as to an investor's tax liability. In order to ascertain the value (and reduce risk that the valuation is challenged by the IRS) of such interests, the taxpayer would benefit from obtaining a third-party appraisal of such interest if the value of such interest may be below the amount of the remaining deferred gain. Nonetheless, such third-party appraisal remains subject to challenge which will cause some taxpayers to overpay tax liability to avoid risk of noncompliance, and others to obtain below market valuations in order to reduce taxation. **Each inclusion event (as well as the inclusion on December 31, 2026) creates a valuation issue with respect to both the valuation of interest itself, and the size of the discounts used for lack of control and lack of marketability.**

Second, to the extent that valuation is less than the remaining deferred gain, the net result to the taxpayer is the equivalent to a recognition of loss with respect to the original deferred gain by the difference between the remaining deferred gain and the fair market value of the interest. Technically, the amount of gain that is included is less than it would have been (so there is no technical recognition of a loss) but the effect is that the taxpayer benefits from the "loss" (by reducing the amount of gain recognized) as a result of holding equity interests (in the QOF) without actually reducing the taxpayer's equity in such investment vehicle. If the investment later becomes valuable, and then sells after the ten-year holding period for a substantial return, the investor would have avoided a substantial portion of the capital gain on the original capital gain (*i.e.*, more than 15-percent of the original capital gain) and all of the capital gain on the disposition after ten years (including no recapture of the additional amounts not recognized at the time of the respective inclusion event).

## ADJUSTMENTS TO THE TAXPAYER'S BASIS IN A QUALIFYING INVESTMENT

§1400Z-2 effectively maintains its own basis rules, independent of regular tax principles.

The taxpayer's basis in a qualifying investment in a QOF is zero,[192] which will be adjusted as provided below:

a. To the extent that a taxpayer includes gain in income under §1400Z-2(a)(1)(B) and §1400Z-2(b)(1), the taxpayer's basis in the investment is increased by such amount of gain so included in the taxpayer's gross income.[193]

b. If a taxpayer holds a qualifying investment for at least five years (*i.e.*, the investment is made on or before December 31, 2021), the basis of such investment is increased by an amount equal to ten-percent of the original deferred gain (which gain was deferred under §1400Z-2(a)(1)).[194]

c.  If a taxpayer holds a qualifying investment for at least seven years (*i.e.*, the investment was made on or before December 31, 2019), the basis of such investment is increased by an amount equal to five- percent of the original deferred gain (which gain was deferred under §1400Z-2(a)(1))[195] (in addition to the 10-percent basis adjustment above).

d.  If a taxpayer holds a qualifying investment for at least ten years, the taxpayer may elect to increase the basis to fair market value at time that the investment is sold or exchanged.[196]

The basis adjustments described above are made immediately after the amount of gain is included in income under §1400Z-2(b)(2)(A).[197] If such basis adjustment is made as a result of an inclusion event, the basis adjustment is made before determining other tax consequences of the inclusion event (*e.g.*, determination of distribution in excess of basis).[198]

A special rule is applicable to gains resulting from a distribution in excess of basis (for corporations, partnerships and S corporations).[199] Specifically, the rule provides in the event of a distribution, any portion of which results in gain resulting from a distribution in excess of basis (determined without regard to a basis adjustment resulting from an inclusion event), (a) such gain is treated as an inclusion event[200] and (b) the taxpayer increases its basis in the qualifying investment before determining the tax consequences of the distribution.[201] The amount of any basis adjustment under §1400Z-2(b)(2)(B)(iii) and (iv) (*i.e.*, the 5-percent and 10-percent basis adjustment) are the only other basis adjustments under the OZ rules.[202]

The Regulations contain additional provisions to reflect rules consistent with the foregoing to apply to partnerships[203] and S corporations, S corporation shareholders and a QOF S Corporation.[204] In the case of partnerships, the normal rules of subchapter K are followed under the Regulations such that debt basis is added to determine the partner's adjusted basis in its partnership interest.[205]

With respect to S corporation shareholders, two modifications are applied:

1. An adjustment to basis of an S corporation's qualifying investment (with regard to the five-year basis adjustment, seven-year basis adjustment or basis adjustment at disposition following a ten-year holding period) (i) will not be separately stated (as provided by §1366) or (ii) adjust the shareholder's stock under §1367, until the date that an inclusion event occurs with respect to the S corporation's qualifying investment; and

2. Basis adjustments made as a result of an inclusion event are made before determining other tax consequences of such inclusion event.[206]

## NOTIFICATION REQUIREMENTS FOR PASS-THROUGH ENTITIES

Partnerships are required to notify partners of the partnership's deferral election and the partner's share of the eligible gain in accordance with the applicable forms and instructions. Importantly, the partnership is also required to notify the partners, in writing, of its deferral election, including the amount of the eligible gain deferred.[207] If an indirect owner of a QOF partnership or QOF S corporation sells a portion of its partnership interests or shares that result in certain inclusion events,[208] such indirect owner must notify the QOF owner sufficient to enable the QOF owner to recognize an appropriate amount of gain.[209] A QOF partner must also notify a QOF of an election made by such partner under §1400Z-2(c) to adjust the basis of a qualifying QOF partnership interest that is disposed of in a taxable transaction.[210]

It does not appear, however, that a partner must notify the partnership if a transaction occurs that gives rise to an inclusion event (nor must the partner notify the partnership of the amount of gain recognized on December 31, 2026).   There are several key implications from this inconsistent set of rules.  First, some partners that are indirect owners have obligations that will be required for the partnership to file its tax return. This may cause errors, delays or amendments to such tax return.  Second, the partnership is required (irrespective of a §754 election) to make inside basis adjustments with respect to a disposition and election made under §1400Z-2(c).  The partnership will therefore incur time and expense to comply with the regulatory regime on behalf of any such partner.  Such partnership may consider requiring that such partner bear the cost of this additional work in its partnership agreement.  Third, since a partner is not obligated to provide information relating to inclusion events or gain recognized in December 31, 2026, failing to provide such information will prevent the partnership from making any inside basis adjustment with respect   to   such   items   if   such   adjustments   are   appropriate.

# CHAPTER EIGHT

# Gain or Loss for Investments Held for Ten Years

The most significant advantage of an Opportunity Zone investment is that the taxpayer has the option of permanently excluding the post-acquisition gain. Section 1400Z-2(c) provides that if a taxpayer makes an election with respect to a qualifying investment held for at least ten years, the basis of such property shall be equal to the fair market value of such investment on the date that the investment is sold or exchanged. **There is no limit to the amount of gain that can be excluded as a result of this rule.** The basis adjustment under §1400Z-2(c) is only applicable to that portion of an investment in a QOF for which a gain deferral election was made.[211] Thus, in the case of a mixed-funds investment, a portion of the gain would be tax free under this section, with the remaining portion treated as being disposed of in a taxable transaction. If the disposition after 10 years resulted in a loss, a taxpayer would not make the election since by making such election, the taxpayer's loss would be reduced to zero. Also, the adjustment to fair market value does not apply to a qualifying investment to the extent that a taxpayer previously claimed a loss or a worthlessness deduction for worthless stock under §165(g) with respect to the investment.[212]

It was unclear under the statute how the step up in basis upon disposition of a qualifying investment after the cessation of the qualified opportunity fund program would be treated. The much needed clarification in the Regulations provides that the ability to make an election under §1400Z-2(c) (to step up the basis of a qualifying investment at disposition) may be made until December 31, 2047.[213] Thus, a QOF owner will have until December 31, 2047 to dispose of its investment (or the QOF will have until such date to dispose of property and make the election under the Regulations).[214]

Unlike the rule for gains eligible for capital gains deferral which require a sale to an unrelated party, no such related party rule exists for the sale after 10 years. Accordingly, subject to ordinary gain inclusion rules (*e.g.*, §1239 and §707(b)(2)), a taxpayer may be able to structure the sale of its QOF interests to a related party after 10 years such that the seller would have no tax on the gain, and the related party buyer receives a stepped-up basis in the acquired property.

## BASIS STEP UP AT DISPOSITION (TO ELIMINATE GAIN UPON A SALE OR EXCHANGE)

If the taxpayer sells or exchanges a qualifying investment that it has held for at least ten years, the taxpayer may make the §1400Z-2(c) election (which will allow the taxpayer to step up the value of its investment to fair market value).[215]   However, this election only applies to the sale or exchange of its investment (i.e., the equity interests in a partnership or corporation).[216]   In many cases involving pass-through entities, the underlying assets of the QOF would be sold rather than each equity holder selling its interests.   Thus, without the special rules adopted by the Regulations (described below), in order to obtain the tax benefits of the basis step up, the taxpayer would need to liquidate the investment entity in the same tax year as the gain is recognized to obtain the tax-free treatment. Moreover, this would result in the taxpayer reflecting significant gain and significant loss in the same year.  These extra steps or reporting positions cause unnecessary complexity and potential for noncompliance.

Under the Regulations, the QOF is required to adjust the basis of partnership assets if the QOF partner's basis is adjusted as a result of a §1400Z-2(c) election.[217]   Addressing the issues raised above with the statutory framework, the Regulations provide that a QOF shall adjust the basis of partnership assets in a manner similar to a §743(b) adjustment (which generally applies to adjust the basis of partnership assets upon the sale or exchange of partnership interests assuming a §754 election was in place or the death of a partner) if such partner has disposed of its investment and made the election.[218]  This section applies without regard to the amount of deferred gain that was included in income or the timing of such inclusion event.  This rule underscores the importance of a partner notifying the partnership of its election so that the basis adjustment is properly made.

**Sale of Assets by QOF or QOZB**

The Regulations provide that if a taxpayer held a qualifying investment in a QOF partnership or QOF S corporation for at least 10 years and the QOF, or any partnership that it owned directly, or indirectly through one more partnerships, sell or exchanges property, the taxpayer can elect to exclude from gross income all gains and losses allocable to the qualifying investment (sometimes referred to as the "Asset Sale Election").[219]

A taxpayer making this election is treated as receiving a distribution of cash from the QOF partnership or QOF S Corporation at the end of their taxable year and immediately recontributing the cash to the QOF partnership or QOF S Corporation in exchange for a non-qualifying investment in the same amount.[220] The amount of the post-contribution qualifying investment and non-qualifying investment is based on the underlying values of the QOF's asset at the end of its taxable year pursuant to Regulation §1.704-1(b)(2)(iv) for a QOF partnership or fair market value for a S Corporation.[221] If the investment is a mixed-funds investment prior to the sale or exchange, the deemed distribution is treated as if were made proportionally with respect to the partner's or shareholder's qualifying investment and non-qualifying investment in the QOF partnership[222] (in accordance with the allocation guidance in Reg. §1.1400Z2(b)-1(c)(6)(iv)(B) or the QOF S corporation).[223] These rules are only to be used for purpose of determining the taxpayer's interest that constitute qualifying and non-qualifying investment in the QOF partnership or QOF S Corporation.[224]

The amount of cash that is deemed distributed by and recontributed is equal to (i) the partner's or shareholder's share of net proceeds from all sales and exchanges of property for the taxable year for which an election is made (under Reg. §1.1400Z2(c)-1(b)(2)(ii)(A) and without regard to whether any gain or loss is recognized with regard to such property) minus (ii) all actual distributions of cash by the QOF partnership or QOF S corporation with respect to the sale or exchange that is made within 90 days of the sale or exchange.[225]

Net proceeds, solely for this purpose and in respect of a QOF partnership, are defined as the amount realized from the sale of property less any indebtedness included in the amount realized that would constitute a qualified liability under §1.707-5(a)(6) if the sold or exchanged property been contributed to a lower-tier partnership subject to the debt.[226] For a QOF S Corporation, net proceeds are defined as the amount realized from the sale of property less and indebtedness included in the amount realized that would constitute a qualified liability under §1.707-5(a)(6).[227]

These above rules are only applicable to the extent that net proceeds have not been distributed to the partners or shareholders within 90 days of the sale or exchange. To demonstrate, A made a qualifying investment in a QOF partnership of 50% that sold its assets for their fair market value of $100 and a basis of $40. A's gain is $30, that was all distributed to B. A would make an election under Reg. §1.1400Z2(c)-1(b)(ii)(A) and the entire gain would be excluded. Alternatively, if the partnership did not distribute the gains from the proceeds and has no indebtedness, A would be treated as receiving a cash distribution of $30.

## MAKING THE ELECTION UPON DISPOSITION FOLLOWING TEN YEAR HOLDING PERIOD

Reg. §1.1400Z2(c)-1(b)(2)(ii)(A) provides that the Asset Sale Election is made on the applicable form with the taxpayer's timely filed income tax return, without extensions, for its taxable year in which it wishes to exclude gains and losses of a QOF partnership or QOF S Corporation.[228]

If a QOF partner or a QOF shareholder makes an election under Reg. §1.1400Z2(c)-1(b)(2)(ii), the excess of any gains over losses that is excluded from income is treated as tax-exempt income of the partnership or S corporation for purposes of §705(a)(1)(B) or §1367(a)(1)(A).[229] The rule is not relevant to determining whether an adjustment is required to the accumulated adjustment account of an S corporation.[230]

## Treatment Of Gains By A QOF REIT

Similar to the election available for investors in a pass-through entity, a shareholder of a QOF REIT that receives a capital gains dividend identified with a date (to the extent that the shareholder's shares in the QOF REIT are a qualifying investment) (i) may treat the applicable capital gains dividend as gain from the sale or exchange of a qualifying investment on the date identified; and (ii) has held such qualifying investment in the QOF REIT for at least ten years, the shareholder may apply a zero percent capital gains rate to the capital gains dividend.[231]  A capital gains dividend identified with a date means (a) the amount of capital gains dividend (as defined in §857(b)(3)(B)) and (b) a date that the QOF REIT designates in a notice provided to the shareholder not later than one week after the QOF REIT designates the capital gain dividend pursuant to §857(b)(3)(B).[232]

Additional rules apply in the case of QOF REITs that provide (i) there is no identification permitted if there are no capital gains from the disposition of qualifying property;[233] (ii) designations of capital gains dividends identified with a date must be proportionate for all dividends paid with respect to the taxable year;[234] (iii) undistributed capital gains may be identified with a date for purposes of excluding gain from income for the taxable year;[235] and (iv) the amount of capital gains determined under these rules is determined without regard to any losses that may have been realize on other sales or exchanges of qualified opportunity zone property (but such identified gains may be limited by the aggregate capital gains dividends that may be designated under §857(b)(3)).[236]  A QOF REIT has two choices in determining the amount of gain with a  date that may be identified: (a) the QOF REIT may identify the first day of the taxable year as the date identified with each designated amount for that taxable year;[237]

or (b) the QOF REIT may use the latest date of each transaction (from latest to earliest) on an iterative basis until all capital gains are identified with dates or there are no earlier dates in which the QOF REIT realized long term capital gains.[238]

# CHAPTER NINE

# Qualified Opportunity Funds

The vehicle that is used under the opportunity zone program to provide for reinvestment into low-income communities and allow for tax benefits investors is the "qualified opportunity fund" or "QOF". Section 1400Z-2(d)(1) provides that the term "qualified opportunity fund" means any investment vehicle which is organized as a corporation or partnership for the purposes of investing in QOZP (other than another qualified opportunity fund) that holds at least 90 percent of its assets in QOZP. The 90-percent test is determined by the average of the percentage of the QOZP held by the QOF as measured (A) on the last day of the first six-month period of the taxable year of the QOF, and (B) on the last day of the taxable year of the QOF.

In effect, the statutory framework for the "qualified opportunity fund" created a binary choice between a structure based on a (A) QOF holding

QOZBP or a (B) QOF holding QOZ stock or QOZ partnership interest, which must be treated as a qualified opportunity zone business (QOZB). Note that the term "qualified opportunity zone business property" is distinct from the term "qualified opportunity zone business". **In most cases, the two-tier structure that is structured as a QOZB is preferable. As we will address below, this approach "wins" in most cases since it allows for a QOF to hold cash and financial assets for 2 ½ years (or longer) instead of only 6 months <u>and</u> requires that only 70-percent (instead of 90-percent) of the underlying assets be treated as QOZBP.**

## GENERAL REQUIREMENTS OF A QOF

As provided in the statute, in order to be considered a QOF, such entity must satisfy the following four requirements: (i) be organized as a corporation or partnership; (ii) for the purposes of investing in QOZP; (iii) that holds at least 90-percent of its assets; (iv) in QOZP.

### *Treatment of Entity as Partnership or Corporation*
**Eligible Entities**

The first requirement to be considered a QOF is that the entity must be organized as a corporation or partnership for federal tax purposes. The IRS has clarified that a limited liability company that is treated as a partnership or corporation for federal tax purposes will qualify as a QOF.[239] An entity that is disregarded for income tax purposes (*e.g.*, a single member LLC), however, will not be treated as a partnership or corporation and is therefore not eligible to be a QOF (nor is a disregarded entity eligible to be a QOZ partnership interest or QOZ stock). Likewise, the Regulations reflect that the federal tax treatment of a corporation or partnership will govern such that the following entities are explicitly described as QOFs under the Regulations: S corporations, REITs, RICs and foreign corporations organized in a US possession. The determination of an entity as a partnership or corporation for federal income tax purposes (such that the entity is required to file a tax return reflecting such tax treatment) will be sufficient for QOF status.

Under the Regulations, only entities that are organized under the law of the United States or the law of one of the 50 states, the District of Columbia, or the US Possessions are eligible to be treated as a QOF.[240] The same requirements requiring a domestic entity apply in the case of QOZ partnership interests and QOZ stock. The Regulations explicitly permit a preexisting entity to qualify as a QOF.[241]

An entity organized in a U.S. territory and not in one of the 50 states (or the District of Columbia), may qualify as a QOF only if it is organized to invest in QOZP that relates to a trade or business operated in the US territory in which it is organized.[242] Correspondingly, a QOZB must conduct business in the U.S. territory in which the entity is organized.

**Self-Certification of a QOF**

In order to be treated as a QOF, such entity must self-certify on an annual basis that it meets the respective eligibility requirements.[243] The self-certification is made by filing Form 8996 with the QOF's tax return and certifying that the QOF meets the requirements under the QOZ program. The annual certification reflects that the QOF continues to meet the certification requirements under the QOF program, calculates the penalty (if any) under the 90-percent tangible property test (referred to as the "investment standard" on Form 8996), and details the QOF's qualifying investments. When a QOF no longer can meet the qualification as a QOF, it would be subject to penalties under the investment standard test. To avoid such penalties, a QOF may decertify as a qualified opportunity fund.

The decertification procedure was included in a draft of the 2021 Form 8996 but was not included in the final version of the form. Presumably, the decertification language will be added to future versions of Form 8996.[244]

The Regulations do not provide any explicit relief if a QOF fails to properly self-certify, and therefore is not treated as a QOF. In situations where a QOF failed to File Form 8996 and self-certify as a QOF, a QOF may generally apply for relief under Reg. §301.9100-1 through Reg. §301.9100-1 (general standards to allow an extension of time to make a regulatory election). The IRS has issued many private letter rulings granting relief to QOFs that have failed to make the timely self-certification election and file Form 8996 when such funds were properly advised as to the QOZ treatment and the failure to file was inadvertent.[245]

### . . . Formed for the Purpose of Investing in Qualified Opportunity Zone Property

The second requirement to be a QOF provides that an entity that desires to be a QOF must be formed for the purpose of investing in QOZP.[246] This rule manifests itself by requiring a number of specific requirements under the Code and Regulations. First, a QOF must self-certify as a QOF by filing Form 8996 with their annual tax return[247] in which the QOF (i) identifies the first taxable year that the eligible entity desires to be treated as a QOF;[248] and (ii) identifies the first month the QOF in which the eligible entity wants to be treated as a QOF.[249] **If an investment is made in an eligible entity that will be treated as a QOF, prior to the date that the QOF elects to be treated as a QOF, such investment will not be eligible for gain deferral (and such portion of the investment in the eligible entity will be a non-qualifying investment).**[250] The self-certification is made by filing Form 8996 in which the required information is provided to the Commissioner.

Second, the QOF must certify on Form 8996 that by the end of the taxpayer's first qualified opportunity fund year, the taxpayer's organizing documents must include a statement of the entity's purpose of investing in QOZP and should include the description of the QOZB.[251] The term "organizing documents" is not defined. However, both organization or incorporation documents and partnership/operating agreements are often considered to be "organizing documents". Accordingly, in the absence of further guidance, taxpayers should include such language in the QOF's operating agreement (or comparable agreement for the respective type of entity).[252]

Third, in light of the purpose requirement, a pre-existing entity (*i.e.*, an entity that existing prior to the enactment of the opportunity zone legislation) is expressly permitted to be a QOF, but the eligible entity must satisfy all of the requirements of §1400Z-2, including the requirements regarding QOZP, as defined in §1400Z-2(d)(2) (particularly, that the property must be acquired after December 31, 2017).[253] As a practical point, the QOF can be formed and commence activities prior to the month that it certifies itself as a QOF, however, it should not accept investments prior to that month.

### Ninety Percent Asset Test

Section 1400Z-2(d)(1) provides that a QOF must hold at least 90 percent of its assets in QOZP. §1400Z-2(d)(2)(A) provides that QOZP means property which is (i) QOZBP; (ii) QOZ stock; or (iii) QOZ partnership interest. If an eligible entity self-certifies as a QOF for a month other than the first month of the taxable year, for purposes of the 90 percent testing requirements: (i) the phrase "first 6-month period of the taxable year" of the fund means (i) the first 6 months of the taxable year in which the eligible entity is a QOF or (ii) if the taxable year ends prior to 6 months after the eligible entity is formed, then on the last day of its taxable year.[254]

Thus, if an eligible entity becomes a QOF in seventh month or later in the taxable year, then the 90 percent test of §1400Z-2(d)(1) takes into account only the QOF's assets on the last day of the taxable year;[255] and (ii) the computation of any penalty under §1400Z-2(f)(1) does not take into account any month before the month that the eligible entity becomes a QOF.[256] The testing date rules are illustrated in the below chart (for calendar year entities):

| Month Entity Elects to be QOF | 1st Testing Period | 2nd Testing Period |
| --- | --- | --- |
| January | June 30 | December 31 |
| April | September 30 | December 31 |
| September | December 31 | June 30 of the following year |

After the QOF's first taxable year, a calendar year taxpayer's testing dates are June 30 and December 31.

*In practical terms, a QOF will normally meet the 90-percent investment standard by owning one or more entities that each qualify as a QOZB (and no other material assets), effectively eliminating the application of the 90-percent test at the QOF level.*

**Valuation (for Testing Purposes)**

Under the applicable forms and instructions, Form 8996 provides the mechanism by which the 90-percent test is measured. Under these rules, the test simply measures the average of the percentage for the first testing period, and the percentage of the second period. So long as the average of these two percentages is greater than 90-percent, no penalty will apply. The penalty is computed if the average is below 90-percent. Note that the asset base for each period is not relevant in making this determination.

Under the Regulations a QOF has two choices for valuing its assets for the purpose of the 90-percent test: (1) using the applicable financial statement valuation if the QOF has an applicable financial statement, or (2) the alternative valuation method, which is based on the unadjusted cost basis of the asset under §1012, subject to certain exceptions.[257] During any single taxable year, the QOF must apply a consistent valuation method. The QOF, however, can change its methodology year to year.[258]

1.  The applicable financial statement valuation method provides that the entity will use, for purposes of valuing the tangible property for the 90-percent test, the value set forth on such entity's applicable financial statement (within the meaning of §1.475(a)-4(h)) for the relevant reporting period.[259]

2.  Under the alternative valuation method, the property owned by the QOF that is purchased or constructed for fair market value is the unadjusted basis of the asset under §1012 or §1013.[260] All other property that is not purchased or constructed for fair market value is determined by the property's fair market value as of each testing date.[261]

If the QOF uses the applicable financial statement method and, those statements, assign a value to the lease, the lease will be valued based on the reported value.[262] If the statements do not assign a value to leases, the alternative valuation method must be used.

Under the alternative valuation method, value of a leased asset is the present value of the leased asset.[263] The present value that will be used for all future testing dates is the sum of the present values of each payment under lease as calculated at the time the QOF enters into it.[264] The payments are discounted using the applicable federal rate under

§1274(d)(1), based on semiannual compounding, for the month in which the QOF enters the lease.[265]

In the valuation of a lease, the term of the lease includes periods during which the lessee may extend the lease at a pre-defined market rate rent.[266] For nonresidential real property or residential real property, pre-defined market rate rent does not include the option to renew at a fair market value that would be determined at the time of the renewal. The pre-defined rent is included in the calculation of the lease payments only if the terms are market rate at the time the lease entered into, reflecting common, arm's-length pricing in the geographic location that includes the QOZ as determined under §482.[267] There will be a rebuttable presumption that the terms of the extension of the lease are market rate for leases not between related parties.[268]

The Regulations also provide various taxpayer-friendly rules that allow the following assets to be disregarded for the purpose of the 90-percent asset test:

- the value of all inventory (including raw materials) of the trade or business[269]; and

- the value of property contributed within six months of the testing date if all of the following conditions are met (i) the property was received by a QOF partnership as a contribution or by a QOF corporation solely in exchange for stock of the corporation; (ii) the contribution or exchange occurred not more than 6 month before the relevant testing date; and (iii) between the date of the 5th business day after the contribution or exchange and the date of the semiannual test, the amount was held continuously in cash, cash equivalents, or debt instrument with a term of 18 months or less.[270] Importantly, the QOF does not need to be consistent from one semi-annual test to the next if it uses this six-month exception option.[271]

**The effect of the six-month rule is to allow for a QOF that operates its business through directly owned QOZBP to hold cash for up to six months without being treated as failing to hold QOZ property.** A QOZB does not need to utilize this rule since it may avail itself of the 31-month working capital safe harbor (described in more detail below).

Section 1400Z-2(e)(4)(B) authorizes Treasury to issue regulations to ensure that a QOF has a reasonable amount of time to reinvest the return of capital from qualified investments and to reinvest proceeds from the sale or disposition of QOZP. The Regulations provide that a QOF will have 12-months to reinvest such proceeds (beginning on the date of the respective distribution, sale or disposition) in QOZP, without running afoul of the 90-percent asset test.[272]   Under this rule, the testing requirements will not be affected if the proceeds are held in cash, cash equivalents or debt instruments with a term of 18 months or less. As with the working capital safe harbor, if reinvestment of the proceeds is delayed due to waiting for governmental action (so long as the application has been completed with respect to such action) such delay does not cause a failure of the 12-month reinvestment requirement.

## OPERATING A QOF (DIRECTLY OR THROUGH A QUALIFIED OPPORTUNITY ZONE BUSINESS)

As noted above, a QOF will be operated either through a QOF holding 'qualified opportunity zone business property' directly, or more likely, by owning QOZ stock or QOZ partnership interest that in turn operates as a 'qualified opportunity zone business' (which incorporates the rules applicable to qualified opportunity zone business property). The mechanics of these requirements are discussed below.

## Qualified Opportunity Zone Business Property

The term "qualified opportunity zone business property" means tangible property used in a trade or business of the qualified opportunity fund if the following requirements are satisfied:

1. ***Acquisition Test.*** Such property was acquired by the QOF by purchase (as defined in §179(d)(2)) after December 31, 2017;

2. ***Original Use or Substantial Improvement Test.*** The original use of the property in the QOZ commences with the QOF or the QOF substantially improves the property; and

3. ***Substantially All Test(s).*** During *substantially all* of the QOF's holding period for such property, *substantially all* of the use of such property was in a QOZ.[273]

Tangible property used in a trade or business of a QOF is QOZBP if the requirements set forth below are satisfied: [274]

## Acquired by Purchase (or Lease)...

The first test is that the property must be acquired *by purchase* after December 31, 2017. In this regard, the term "purchase" means any acquisition of property, but only if (A) the property is not acquired from a related party (as defined in §267 or §707(b));[275] (B) the property is not acquired by one component member of a controlled group from another component member of the same controlled group, and (C) the basis of the property in the hands of the acquiring party is not determined (i) in whole or in part by reference to the adjusted basis of the transferring party or (ii) under §1014 (relating to property acquired from a decedent). Moreover, the Regulations add the requirement (which is already implicit by reference to §179(d)(2)) that the property must be acquired from an unrelated party (within the meaning of §1400Z-2(e)(2) and which defines related party by reference to §267 and §707(b), by substituting "20 percent" for "50 percent" each place in which it appears).[276]

There are no statutory restrictions on acquiring leasehold interests in property (including from a related party). The Regulations provide much broader latitude in obtaining leasehold interests in property as compared to acquiring property by purchase. To that end, the Regulations effectively allow nearly all leased property to be treated as QOZP, subject to certain limitations to avoid abusive transactions. Below are the rules (and limitations) for treating leased property as QOZP:

1. The leased property acquired by the QOF must be pursuant to a lease entered into after December 31, 2017.[277]

2. The terms of the lease must be market rate (reflecting common, arms-length market practice in the locale that includes the QOZ as determined under §482) at the time that the lease was entered into.[278]

3. If the lessee and lessor are related parties, the (i) the lessee cannot at any time make any prepayment under the lease relating to a period of use that exceeds 12 months; and (ii) if the original use of the property in QOZ[279] does not commence with the lessee, the property is not QOZBP unless, during the relevant testing period,[280] the lessee becomes the owner of tangible property that is QOZBP having a value not less than that leased tangible property.[281] Under this rule, there must be substantial overlap of the zones in which the owner of the property so acquired uses it and the zones in which that person uses the leased property. The effect of this rule is

to prohibit a party that uses non-qualified property in a QOZ to effectively convert it to QOZP by leasing the same property to a related party without otherwise satisfying the qualified property rules. By requiring that such related party must own property with at least the same value as under the related party lease, it reflects that the related party is meeting the intent of the program to reinvest in the QOZ.

*Practice Tip*: Subject to certain anti-abuse provisions, a QOF may lease property (including real property) from a related party and meet the requirements of the QOZ program. Although complicated, this approach may be necessary to allow a party with preexisting land holdings to benefit from the QOZ tax benefits.[282]

## Original Use or Substantial Improvement of Tangible Property Requirement

The second test requires that either (i) the original use of tangible property will commence with the QOF or that such property is substantially improved by the QOF (or the QOZB).

### *Original Use Requirement*

If the original use of tangible property commences with the QOF under §1400Z-2(d)(2)(D), such property will meet the test to be treated as QOZBP (subject to the acquisition rules in addition to the holding period and usage requirements).

Under the Regulations, the following rules apply to determine whether property satisfies the original use requirement.

**General Rule (Placed in Service Requirement)**. The original use of tangible property in a QOZ commences on the date that any person first places property in service in the QOZ for purposes of depreciation and amortization (or first uses it in a manner that would allow depreciation or amortization if that person was the property's owner).[283]

*Planning Tip*: As a result of this rule, a real estate development project may be full constructed and then sold to a QOF prior to being placed in service, and meet the criteria as QOZBP for purposes of the QOZ program.

**Vacant, Brownfields and Certain Acquired Property**. If the property has been unused or vacant for an uninterrupted period of (1) at least one calendar year beginning on a date in which the property was designated a QOZ and has been vacant through the date that the property was purchased or (2) for three calendar years if it became vacant after the location of the property was designated a QOZ, its original use in the zone commences on the date after the period when any person first uses or places the property in service in the QOZ (within the meaning of the preceding paragraph).[284]

Real property, including land and buildings will be considered in a state of vacancy if the property is significantly unused (*i.e.*, more than 80-percent of the building or land, as measured by square footage or usable space, is not currently being used.[285]

Any property designated as a brownfield site under Section 101 of 42. US.C. 9601 may treat all property comprising the brownfield site as satisfying the original use test if the entity meets basic safety standards.[286] Also, property that is acquired from a local government by purchase, which was obtained by the local government as a result of an involuntary conversion, will be treated as satisfying the original use test.[287]

**Used Property**.    Used tangible property satisfies the original use requirement if the property has not been previously so used or placed in service in the QOZ (if it had been so used, it must be substantially improved in order to be treated as QOZBP).[288]

In light of these rules, a QOF business could fail this standard if it acquires used equipment that will not be substantially improved. Although most businesses use new equipment, certain businesses utilize used equipment (*e.g.*, heavy construction equipment, vehicles, restaurant equipment) to save costs. Such businesses should examine their proposed business plan in light of the QOF rules.

**Leased Property**. The improvements made by a lessee to leased property satisfy the original use requirement as purchased property for the amount of unadjusted cost basis under §1012 of such improvements.[289]

**Property Leased to a Related Party**. In a related party lease arrangement, the original use of the leased tangible property in the opportunity zone commences on the date that any person first places the property in service in the QOZ for the purposes of depreciation or amortization (or first uses it in a manner that would allow depreciation and amortization if the person was the property's owner).[290] Used leased property may satisfy the original use requirement if such property has not previously been used in the qualified opportunity zone.

**Leased Real Property**. In the case of real property (other than unimproved land) that is leased by a QOF, if, at the time that the lease was entered into, there was a plan, intent or expectation for the real property to be purchased by the QOF for an amount of consideration other than the fair market value of the real property (determined at the time of purchase without regard to prior lease payments), the leased real property is not treated as QOZBP.[291]

*Substantial Improvement*

In general, to qualify as QOZBP, such property must be substantially improved by the QOF.[292] Property is treated as substantially improved by the QOF only if, during the 30 month period beginning after the date of acquisition of such property, additions to basis with respect to such property in the hands of the QOF exceed an amount equal to the adjusted basis of such property at the beginning of such 30 month period.[293] In other words, the cost of improvements must exceed the cost (or adjusted basis) of such property. However, if a QOF purchases a building located on land wholly within a QOZ, a substantial improvement to the purchased tangible property is measured by the QOF's adjusted basis to the building.[294] For purposes of measuring whether the QOF meets the substantial improvement test, the QOF is not required to separately substantially improve the land upon which the building is located.[295]

This rule is illustrated in Rev. Rul. 2018-29 by describing a situation in which a QOF acquires property for $800K (located wholly in a QOZ) which consists of land (valued at $480K) and a vacant factory (valued at $320K).[296] Over the following 24 months, the QOF invests $400K to convert the building to a residential rental property. The ruling held that the substantial improvement is measured solely by the additions to the basis of the building and not the land, and that the foregoing example met the substantial improvement test. The fact that no improvements were made to the land reflects the rule that a QOF is not required to separately substantially improve the land upon which the building is located. Unimproved land that is within a QOZ and acquired by purchase is not required to be substantially improved.[297] Rather, the land will be treated as QOZBP immediately (so long as the other requirements under the QOZ program are satisfied).

*Treatment of Property During Working Capital Safe Harbor Period*

The Regulations provided one of the most taxpayer-friendly rules for QOZs by providing flexibility during the working capital safe harbor period. An entity that otherwise satisfies the working capital safe harbor will generally be treated as meeting the 70-percent tangible property test during the safe harbor period.[298]

If property of an entity that would otherwise be treated as nonqualified financial property (*e.g.*, cash) as being a reasonable amount of working capital because the entity meets the working capital safe harbor requirements, the *entity* is considered to have satisfied the requirement of §1400Z-2(d)(3)(A)(i) (referring to the requirement that substantially all tangible property is QOZBP) during such working capital safe harbor period.[299] Thus, if the QOZB's property is viewed in the aggregate, it will be deemed to satisfy the tangible property requirement during the working capital safe harbor period. Accordingly, a QOZB may avail itself of either of the foregoing exceptions such that it will be treated as satisfying the tangible property tests during the working capital safe harbor period(s) and, by the end of such period, when it is required to satisfy the tangible property tests (including newly constructed property), it is anticipated that such entity will satisfy the 70-percent test.

**As a result of this rule, a QOZB may improve nonqualified property during the working capital safe harbor period and, so long as the 70-percent test is met at the end of the working capital safe harbor period, the entity will be considered to have met the 70-percent standard from inception.**

*Aggregation Rules*

The Regulations contain various aggregation rules in the context of the substantial improvement requirements.

The first rule generally permits cost of qualified property to be taken into account in determining the additions to basis of non-original use property (and such property must satisfy the standard under the substantial improvement test rather than the original use test).[300] The effect of this rule is to allow nonqualified property to be converted to qualified property with the additions to basis even if it would have been nonqualified under the original use test alone, and the original use property acquired by the QOZB will not be treated as original use property but rather additions to basis of substantial improvement property.

The second aggregation rule effectively permits buildings to be aggregated to determine whether an entity satisfies the substantial improvement test if such buildings qualify as an "eligible building group".[301] Such term will apply to each building located within the geographic borders of a parcel of land described in a single deed. Moreover, this rule may be applies across contiguous parcels described in separate deeds if certain requirements are met.[302]

### Special Rules for Land and Improvements to Land

The Regulations provide for a special rule pertaining to land in the context of the substantial improvement tests. For this purpose, if a building located within the geographic boundaries of a QOZ is purchased, the entity's additions to basis are determined under §1012.[303] Unimproved land within a QOZ and acquired by purchase is not required to be substantially improved.[304] Nevertheless, if land is only unimproved or minimally improved and there is no intention to improve the land within 30 months by more than an insubstantial amount, then such land is not considered QOZBP.[305] In determining whether an entity had an expectation or intention to improve the land by more than an insubstantial amount, improvements to the land by the entity (including grading, clearing of land, remediation and purchase of other property that facilitates the use o the land in a trade or business) will be taken into account. Also under these rules, remediation costs that are treated as betterments to the property may be added to basis for purposes of the substantial improvement rules.[306] The Regulations explicitly note that there is no requirement that land must be substantially improved when determining whether a building has been substantially improved under the applicable tests.[307]

## Substantially All

The third test for property to be treated as QOZBP is that during substantially all of the QOF's holding period for such property, substantially all of the use of such property was in a QOZ. [308] Since the holding period requires that during such time, the QOZBP must be used in a trade or business, this test effectively incorporates a trade or business requirement as well.

### Holding Period Requirement

Be aware that this rule contains two different tests, for two different uses of the term "substantially all". The first requirement relates to the QOF's holding period. The second requirement relates to the use of property in a QOZ. In this regard, the term 'substantially all of the QOF's holding period' means during at least 90-percent of the QOF's holding period.[309] However, the term 'substantially all of the usage of tangible property by a QOF in a QOZ requires at least 70-percent of the use of tangible property in a QOZ.[310]

For a discussion of the "use" of property in the QOZ, see discussion below in Chapter 10 (relating to use requirement for a QOZB).

### Trade or Business Requirement

In order to be treated as QOZBP, such property must be used in the trade or business of a QOF (in order to satisfy the "use" requirement). For this purpose, the term "trade or business" means a trade or business within the meaning of §162.[311] In general, §162 refers to the deductibility of business expenses providing that a taxpayer is allowed a deduction for all ordinary and necessary expenses paid or incurred in carrying on a trade or business.[312] However, the term "trade or business", despite being used in nearly 500 separate subsections of the Code and nearly 700 separate Treasury Regulations, has not been defined under the Code, Regulations or by the IRS for purposes of §162. Rather, case law drives the determination of what constitutes a §162 trade or business.

The evolution of case law in this area culminated in the determination in *Groetzinger v. Commissioner* in which the Supreme Court held that the taxpayer was engaged in a trade or business when the following factors were met: (i) the activity must be conducted for profit; (ii) the activity must be engaged in with some regularity and continuity (even if not by the taxpayer personally); and (iii) the taxpayer must have commenced operations.[313]

The courts have consistently applied any applicable tests to the facts and circumstances of each situation. In this regard, the determination of whether an activity constitutes a trade or business is based on the facts and circumstances.[314]

Under the Regulations, the "use" requirement will only be satisfied to the extent that a QOF operates a trade or business. Accordingly, the mere holding of property without conducting an activity that is considered a trade or business under §162 will fail the substantially all test under the Statute and Regulations. *See* discussion on triple net leases below in Chapter 10 (relating to the trade or business requirement of a QOZB).

# QUALIFIED OPPORTUNITY ZONE BUSINESS

The other manner in which a qualified opportunity zone may be run in compliance with the QOZ program is to operate a qualified opportunity zone business. Under the Regulations, significant tax payer-friendly and flexible criteria were added to qualified opportunity zone businesses, making the program much more user friendly. QOZBs are discussed at length in the next chapter.

The threshold requirement to operate an opportunity zone business is that the equity interests held by the QOF must consist of either QOZ stock or QOZ partnership interest (each of which must be operated as a QOZB). Note that a QOZB must hold at least 70-percent of its assets as QOZBP, and the QOZB must satisfy this test.

## *Qualified Opportunity Zone Stock*

Qualified opportunity zone stock means any stock in a *domestic* corporation if:[315]

(i)     such stock is acquired by the QOF after December 31, 2017, at its original issue (directly or through an underwriter) from the corporation solely in exchange for cash;[316]

(ii)    as of the time that such stock was issued, such corporation was a QOZB (or, in the case of a new corporation, such corporation was being organized for the purpose of being a QOZB); and

(iii)   during *substantially all* (*i.e.*, at least 90-percent)[317] of the QOF's holding period for such stock, such corporation qualified as a QOZB.

The first requirement of the statute is that the QOF acquires the QOZ stock solely in exchange for cash (see below for the comparable rule in the case of partnerships). While the Regulations permit the contribution of property to be treated as a qualifying investment, this is not contemplated by the statutory text. To that end, a QOF may acquire QOF Stock first for cash and then subsequently contribute property to avoid running afoul of the explicit language of the statute.[318] Thus, capitalizing a QOZB will be two-step process if it will be capitalized property other than cash (with the cash originally issued in exchange for equity, followed by property contributions).

Under the statute, rules similar to §1202(c)(3) (with respect to certain redemptions) apply for purposes of determining whether stock in a corporation qualifies as QOZ stock. Specifically, this provision provides that certain redemptions will cause the acquired stock to not be treated as qualified stock (in the case of §1202, for qualified small business stock). Regulation §1.1400Z-2(d)-1(c)(2)(ii) clarifies this rule (consistent with the requirements of §1202(c)(3)) such that:

(A) stock acquired by the QOF is not treated as QOZ stock if, during the four year time period beginning two years before the issuance of such stock, the issuing corporation purchased (directly or indirectly) any of its stock from the QOF or from a person related (within the meaning of §267(b) or §707(b)) to the QOF.[319]

(B) stock issued by the corporation is not treated as QOZ stock if, during the two year time period beginning one years before the issuance of such stock, the issuing corporation purchased (directly or indirectly) an aggregate of five percent of the value of the stock (as of the beginning of the two year period).[320]

(C) if any transaction is treated under §304(a) as a distribution in redemption of stock of any corporation, such corporation is treated as purchasing an amount of its stock equal to the amount that is treated as a distribution under §304(a).[321]

## Qualified Opportunity Zone Partnership Interest

Qualified opportunity zone partnership interest means any capital or profits interest in a *domestic* partnership if: [322]

(i)     such partnership interest is acquired by the QOF after December 31, 2017, from the partnership solely in exchange for cash;[323]

(ii)    as of the time that such partnership interest was acquired, such partnership was a QOZB (or, in the case of a new corporation, such partnership was being organized for the purpose of being a QOZB); and

(iii)   during *substantially all* (*i.e.*, at least ninety percent)[324] of the QOF's holding period for such partnership interest, such partnership qualified as a QOZB.

As with QOZ stock, the statute requires that a QOF must acquire the QOZ partnership interests solely in exchange for cash. Thus, the equity interests of the QOZ partnership interests should be acquired for at least a nominal amount of cash (proportionately by the equity holders of such entity) prior to any subsequent contribution of property to comply with the           language           of           the           statutory           text.[325]

# CHAPTER TEN

# Qualified Opportunity Zone Businesses

The QOZ legislation has a substantial structural flaw in that it creates different treatment for a QOF that operate its business directly (through the ownership of 90-percent or more of its assets consisting of QOZP) rather than through QOZ stock or QOZ partnership interests (as the case may be). In the case of QOZ stock or QOZ partnership interests, such corporation or partnership must meet the requirements of a "qualified opportunity zone business" or QOZB.

**In most cases, the treatment as QOZB is desirable since (i) the QOZP owned or leased by the QOZB must exceed 70-percent (rather than 90-percent) of the total property owned or leased by**

**such entity; and (ii) the QOZB may avail itself of the working capital safe harbor.**

A QOZB means a trade or business (i) in which substantially all of the tangible property owned or leased by the taxpayer is QOZBP; (ii) which satisfies certain requirements relating to the active conduct of a trade or business, as well as holding requirements with respect to nonqualified financial property; and (iii) does not consist of any of the following trades or businesses (or providing the land for such businesses): private or commercial golf course, massage parlor, hot tub facility, suntan facility, racetrack or other facility used for gambling, or liquor stores (with a principal business for consumption off the premises) (the foregoing, collectively, are referred to as 'sin' businesses).[326]

Since the second of these requirements (relating to criteria described in §1397) contains three separate requirements, to meet the definition of a QOZB, such QOZ partnership or QOZ corporation must meet *five* separate requirements:

1. **70-percent QOZBP Requirement.** At least 70-percent of the tangible property owned by the QOZB is QOZBP;

2. **50-percent Active Trade or Business Requirement.** At least 50-percent of the total gross income of such entity is derived from the active conduct of a trade or business;

3. **Use of Intangible Property in Trade or Business.** At least 40-percent of the intangible property is used in the active conduct of the business;

4. **Limitation on Nonqualified Financial Property**. Less than 5-percent of the aggregate adjusted bases of property is attributable to nonqualified financial property; and

5. **Certain Business Prohibited**. The business does not consist of 'sin' businesses.

Tangible property of a QOZB that ceases to be QOZBP will continue to be treated as QOZBP for the lesser of (i) 5 years after the date that the property ceased being so qualified, or (ii) the date on which the tangible property is no longer held by the QOZB.[327]

## SUBSTANTIALLY ALL REQUIREMENT

The first component is met when substantially all of the property meets the tests to be treated as QOZBP. For these purposes, the term "substantially all" means at least 70-percent of the tangible property used or leased by the trade or business is QOZBP.[328] The QOZB's percentage is calculated using the applicable financial statement valuation method, if the entity has an applicable financial statement, [329] or the alternative valuation method.[330]

When valuing tangible property for the 70-percent QOZBP requirement, if a taxpayer self-certified as a QOF and holds an equity interest in an eligible entity that is tested as a QOZB, the taxpayer may value the eligible entity using the same valuation methodology that it uses for determining its own compliance with the 90-percent investment standard, if no other equity holder in the eligible entity is a five-percent zone taxpayer.[331] When there two or more five percent zone taxpayers in the QOF that invests in the QOZB, the value of the QOZB's tangible property can be calculated by applying the compliance methodology of any of the five percent zone taxpayers.[332]

While the manner in which the holding period is determined is clear, the determination of the "use" requirement requires interpretation. Accordingly, the Regulations focus the respective rules on the manner in which a QOF or QOZB will meet the "use" requirement under the substantially all test.

A QOF has satisfied the substantially all threshold (relating to the required 70-percent usage of tangible property in a zone) if not less than 70-percent of the total utilization of the tangible property occurs at a location within the geographic borders of an opportunity zone.[333]

*Safe Harbor for Businesses Rendering Services.* In meeting these requirements, the following safe harbor applies to business that provide services (to determine whether property will satisfy the 70-percent property standard):[334]

1. The tangible property utilized in rendering the service generates gross income for the trade or business both inside and outside the geographic borders of a QOZ;

2. The trade or business has an office or other facility located within the QOZ;

3. The tangible property is operated by employees of the trade or business who (1) regularly use the QOZ office of the trade or business and (2) are managed directly, actively and substantially, on a day-to-day basis by one or more employees who carry out their duties at a QZ office; and

4. The tangible property is not operated exclusively outside of a qualified opportunity zone for a period longer than 14 consecutive days for the generation of gross income for the trade or business.

For purposes of the 70-percent property standard, this safe harbor may not be used to treat more than 20-percent of the tangible property of the trade or business as qualified tangible property.[335]

*Safe Harbor for Tangible Property Owned by Leasing Businesses with QOZ Offices.* Tangible property of a trade or business, the employees of which use to regularly lease such tangible property to customers of the trade or business, may be treated as qualified property if:[336]

1. Consistent with normal, usual or customary conduct of the trade or business, when not subject to a lease to customers, such tangible property is parked or otherwise stored at a QOZ office; and

2. No lease under which a customer of the trade or business acquires possession of tangible property is for a duration (including extensions) of not more than 30 consecutive days.

Since the definition of a QOZB includes the requirement that substantially all of the tangible property owned or leased is QOZBP, the rules applicable to QOZBP described in Chapter 9 above will apply to such property.

1. The valuation rules of Reg. §1.1400Z2(b)(2)(ii)(A) are also adapted from rules issued with respect to QOZBP. In this regard, whether a trade or business satisfies the 70-percent substantially all threshold is determined by the following fraction:

**Total Value of All QOZBP Owned or Leased by The QOF (Which Is Qualifying Property)**

## Total Value of All Tangible Property Owned or Leased By The QOF, Whether Located Inside or Outside of a Zone.[337]

2.  The Regulations adopt the general rule that the value of owned or leased tangible property is valued under either the applicable financial statement valuation method or the alternative valuation method. The chosen method must be consistent for each taxable year.[338] The applicable financial statement valuation method provides that the entity will use, for purposes of valuing the tangible property for the 70-percent test, the value set forth on such entity's applicable financial statement.[339] The "applicable financial statement" method may only be used if such applicable financial statement is prepare under GAAP, and would otherwise require, an assignment of value to the lease of tangible property.[340]

3.  Under the alternative valuation method (i) the value of tangible property that is owned by the QOZB is the unadjusted cost basis of the property under §1012 in the hands of the QOZB for each testing date of a QOF during the year;[341] and (ii) the value of tangible property that is leased by the QOZB is equal to the present value of the leased tangible property.[342] For purposes of this rule, the acquisition by a QOF of QOZ Stock or QOF partnership interest is treated as a purchase of such interest by the QOF. The present value of the leased tangible property is (1) equal to the sum of the present values of each payment under the lease for such property; (2) calculated at the time that the QOZB enters into the lease for such leased tangible property; and (3) used as the value for such asset by the QOZB for all testing dates for purposes of the 90-percent asset test. The discount rate used for these purposes is the discount rate set forth in §1274(d)(1) (by substituting the term "lease" for "debt instrument"). The lease term used for these purposes is the original lease term including extensions at a pre-defined rent.

Under these valuation rules, the value of each property that is not purchased or constructed is the property's fair market value, and is determined on the first 6-month period of the taxable year, and the last day of the taxable year. [343] This rule has the effect of requiring any partnership interest or other intangible interest (including a carried interest in an underlying entity) to be valued at fair market value for purposes of the 90-percent test, on each testing date.

# 50-PERCENT GROSS INCOME TEST

## Active Conduct of Trade or Business

The second requirement is that at least 50 percent of the total gross income of such entity is derived from the active conduct of such business in the QOZ (or multiple QOZs).[344]  The Regulations provide four tests that an entity may use to determine whether it meets the 50 percent threshold.  In this regard, the entity will satisfy the requirement if any of the four tests are met.

Effectively, the active conduct rule requires that an entity (1) meets the definition of a "trade or business" under §162 and (2) satisfies at least one of the safe harbor tests.

**At a high-level, the tests to determine active conduct of a trade or business in a QOZ are fairly broad and provide enough flexibility to capture nearly any type of business (with a facts and circumstances test as an additional safety net).    That said, the administrative burden to track hours and compensation for all workers, including independent contractors providing services to a QOF or QOZB may be overly burdensome.   These rules can therefore create an additional compliance challenge for a business that conducts an operating business (even while affording greater flexibility).**

## Treatment as a "Trade or Business" (Including Discussion of Triple Net Leases)

The Regulations provide that certain activities will not be considered the active conduct of a trade or business. For purposes of this rule, the ownership and operation (including leasing) of real property is the active conduct of a trade or business.[345] However, merely entering into a triple net lease with respect to real property owned by the taxpayer is not the active conduct of a trade or business by such taxpayer.[346] The term trade or business is defined (as it is elsewhere for opportunity zone purposes) as having the same meaning that such term has under §162.[347]

Section 162(a) permits a taxpayer, including a corporation, to deduct ordinary and necessary expenses paid or incurred in carrying on a trade or business.[348] Section 162 expenses are fully deductible from gross income. A trade or business expense is ordinary for such purpose if it is normal or customary within a particular trade, business, or industry, and it is necessary if it is appropriate and helpful for the development of the business.[349]

The phrase "trade or business" is not defined in the Code or the Treasury Regulations. However, the Supreme Court has stated there are three requirements for an activity to constitute a trade or business: (i) the activity must be conducted for profit; (ii) the activity must be engaged in with some regularity and continuity (even if not by the taxpayer personally); and (iii) the taxpayer must have commenced operations.[350]

In the context of rental real estate, the tax court has permitted a single family rental to be treated as a trade or business.[351] A landlord that owned and managed apartment buildings (even through an agent that performed the work) would qualify as a trade or business.[352] However, a triple net lease was not afforded such treatment. Rather, the Tax Court has held that simply renting a property and collecting rents without more does not rise to the level of a trade or business.[353]

Prior to regulations and notices issued for other purposes of the TCJA, the IRS and courts have had a few occasions to address the treatment of triple net leases. Under §871, there are special rules for the taxation of nonresident aliens who are engaged in trade and business in the United States. Revenue Ruling 73-522 provides that a rental under a net lease is not considered a trade or business for the purposes of §871.

In a case in the 7th Circuit Court of Appeals, the court determined whether certain "trades or businesses" would be treated as a single employer for purposes in the context of a dispute over pension withdrawal liability.[354] The taxpayer in that case owned several properties subject to triple net leases. As a result of the properties being subject to triple net leases, the taxpayer only spent five hours per year involved with the properties. Therefore, the court held that "mere holding of leases for ten years by shareholder was not such continuous and regular activity as to constitute a trade or business". In deciding a similar issue, the same court reached the opposite conclusion holding that the taxpayer was much more frequently engaged in activities related to leasing such as buying and selling multiple properties annually, and advertising such properties, and was therefore deemed to have engaged in conduct that was regular and continuous.[355]

Treasury recently released Final Regulations with respect to the qualified business income deduction under §199A. Like the QOZ rules, the §199A rules do not permit the deduction with respect to triple net leases that do not rise to the level of a trade or business under §162. The IRS issued Notice 2019-7 providing for a safe harbor reflecting when rental activities are considered a trade or business. Under this Notice, rental services include advertising to rent, negotiating and executing leases, verifying tenant applications, collection of rent, daily operation and maintenance, management of the real estate, purchase of materials, and supervision of employees and independent contractors. The term rental services does not include financial or investment management activities, such as arranging financing; procuring property; studying and reviewing financial statements or reports on operations; planning, managing, or constructing long-term capital improvements; or hours spent traveling to and from the real estate.

Under the Notice (similar to QOZ rules), real estate that is rented or leased under a triple net lease is not eligible for the safe harbor. A triple net lease includes a lease agreement that requires the tenant or lessee to pay taxes, fees, and insurance, and to be responsible for maintenance activities for a property in addition to rent and utilities (including a lease agreement that requires the payment of such tenant or lessee's allocable portion of taxes, fees insurance and maintenance).

In determining whether a rental real estate activity is a §162 trade or business, relevant factors might include, but are not limited to (i) the type of rented property (commercial real property versus residential property), (ii) the number of properties rented, (iii) the owner's or the owner's agents day-to-day involvement, (iv) the types and significance of any ancillary services provided under the lease, and (v) the terms of the lease (for example, a net lease versus a traditional lease and a short-term lease versus a long-term lease). A number of commentators believe that having multiple triple net leases may rise to the level of a trade or business even where a single lease will likely not meet the standard.

The QOZ Regulations provide two examples to illustrate when a triple-net lease qualifies or fails to qualify as an active trade or business. In the first regulatory example, the lease is to a single tenant. The lessee is responsible for all of the costs related to a leased building (*e.g.*, paying all taxes, insurance, and maintenance expenses) in addition to paying rent, and the lease is considered triple-net. In this example, a triple-net lease to a single tenant is not the active conduct of a trade or business, regardless of whether the lessor maintains an office in the leased space to address issues that may arise with the lease.[356]

On the other hand, in the second regulatory example, the lease is to two or more tenants. The lessor leases a portion of a building on a triple-net basis and other portions under leases that are not triple-net and the lessor maintains an office in the building with employees who are managing and operating the spaces that are not triple-net-leased. This is considered the active conduct of a trade or business.[357]

Arguably, if the lessor pays taxes or insurance, this technically makes the lease no longer triple net. However, there is no guarantee the IRS would not still challenge it if what the IRS is looking for, in terms of "active conduct," is ongoing involvement with the property. Similarly, nearly maintaining the building may not be sufficient to avoid triple-net lease treatment. The maintenance activities would avoid "net" classification only if the lessee was not reimbursing the lessor for those activities. The safest course is for the lessor to retain some level of involvement with the property at the maintenance, management or operational level that is not reimbursed by the lessee, so that the lessor is not "merely" entering into a triple-net lease. If expenses are intended to be passed on to the tenant, a QOZB may want to consider coming up with a rough estimate of those costs and building those amounts into fixed lease payments. In this way, such QOZB will be at risk for increases in these costs (e.g., increased insurance premiums or taxes), which may be an important factor in defeating triple net lease characterization.

## *Safe Harbor Tests*

Treasury issued four tests intended to provide taxpayers with clarity to meet the 50-percent gross income standard. Although the tests are by no means perfect, they provide adequate parameters to eliminate risk of noncompliance in most cases. Moreover, there is enough flexibility to allow close cases to qualify under the QOZ program.

## The Hours Test

A QOZB will meet the threshold if at least 50-percent of the services performed for the trade or business are performed in the opportunity zone (the "Hours Test").[358] The Hours Test is calculated by dividing (1) the total number of hours performed by employees, partners, independent contractors, and employees of independent contractors, for services performed in a QOZ during the taxable year, by (2) the total number of hours performed by employees, partners, independent contractors, and employees of independent contractors, for services performed during the taxable year (in any location).[359] Any amounts paid to partners are taken into account (in the numerator and denominator) to the extent the amounts are considered guaranteed payments for services provided to the partnership under §707(c).[360]

## The Compensation Test

A QOZB will satisfy the test if at least 50-percent of the services performed for a trade or business based on the amounts paid for such services are in a QOZ. (the "Compensation Test").[361] The Compensation Test is measured by determining the fraction, the numerator of which is (1) the total amount paid by the entity for services performed in a QOZ during the taxable year, whether by employees, partners, independent contractors, or employees of independent contractors, and (2) the denominator of which is the total amount paid by the entity for services performed during the taxable year whether by employees, partners, independent contractors, or employees of independent contractors (regardless of the location).[362]

**Tangible Property Safe Harbor**

A QOZB will satisfy the test if the tangible property of the trade or business located in a QOZ and the management or operational functions performed in a QOZ are each necessary for the generation of at least 50-percent of the gross income of the trade or business.[363] This test is less definitive, but presumably would be measured by the rental or other operating income derived from the tangible property, together with an appropriate allocation of management and operational functions performed in a zone.

The Regulations provide an example of the Tangible Property Safe Harbor when a landscaping business has its headquarters and performs its management functions in a QOZ and, additionally, its equipment and supplies are stored in the headquarters facility.[364] The fact that the actual services are performed outside the QOZ is not a relevant factor. On the other hand, where a business has a PO Box in a QOZ and the mail received is fundamental to the business, but there is no other basis for concluding that the income of the trade or business is derived from the activities in the zone, the test would not be met.[365]

**Facts & Circumstances Test**

A QOZB may determine, based on the facts and circumstances that at least 50-percent if the gross income of a QOZB is derived from the active conduct of a trade or business in a QOZ.[366]

The Regulations provide an example, in a situation in which the trade or business derived no gross income for a number of years, had no employees and did not pay for services (*i.e.*, in the case of a real estate development), so long as the taxpayer prior to such time has otherwise complied with the requirements for a QOZB (*e.g.*, has written plans to acquire land in which it plans to construct a building for lease to other trades or businesses as required under the working capital safe harbor rules discussed below), the taxpayer satisfies the facts and circumstances test.[367]  In this example, the QOZB ultimately leased the constructed building and derived more than 50-percent of the entity's gross income from the rental of the property in the QOZ.

## USE OF INTANGIBLE PROPERTY

The third requirement is that a substantial portion of the intangible property of such entity is used in the active conduct of the trade or business in a QOZ.[368]  For purposes of this rule, the term "substantial portion" means at least 40 percent.[369] For the purposes of the test, intangible property will be treated as used in the active conduct of a trade or business in a QOZ if (i) the use of the intangible property is normal, usual or customary in the conduct of the trade or business; and (ii) the intangible property is used in the QOZ in the performance of an activity of the trade or business that contributed to the generation of gross income for the trade or business.[370] The Regulations do not provide any limitation as to the amount of intangible property that the QOZB can own (or lease) as long as it being used in the active conduct of the trade or business.

The final Regulations include a working capital safe harbor providing that intangible property purchased or licensed by the trade or business, pursuant to the reasonable written plan with a written schedule for the expenditure of the working capital, satisfies the use requirement during any period in which the business is proceeding in a manner consistent with the plan.[371] To illustrate this rule, the Regulations provide an example reflecting that during the period of land acquisition and building construction a substantial portion of the taxpayer's intangible property is treated as being used in the active conduct of a trade or business in the QOZ.[372]

## Nonqualified Financial Property and the Working Capital Safe Harbor

The fourth requirement is that less than 5 percent of the average of the aggregate unadjusted bases of the property of such entity is attributable to nonqualified financial property.[373]  The term nonqualified financial property means debt, stock, partnership interests, options, futures contracts, forward contracts, warrants, notional principal contracts, annuities and other similar property, but does not include (1) reasonable amounts of working capital held in cash, cash equivalents or debt instruments with a term or18 months or less; or (2) accounts or notes receivable acquired in the ordinary course of trade or business for services rendered or from the sale property described in §1221(a)(1) (*i.e.*, stock in trade, inventory or property held for sale to customers in the ordinary course of business).[374]  Accordingly, the exception to treatment as nonfinancial property allows a QOZB to (i) hold cash, cash equivalents and short term notes (*i.e.*, working capital assets) and (ii) hold reasonable working capital without violating this rule.[375]

Unfortunately, the inclusion of this rule has the effect of causing certain businesses to fail to qualify as a QOZB.  For example, banks, certain financial management and advisory companies, and other companies that deal with financial products such as mortgage lenders may not qualify since their assets will consist of "bad" assets including nonqualified financial property.  Such businesses could potentially use a single-tier structure (where the QOF owns QOZBP) since the restrictions under §1397C are not applicable.

The Regulations provided latitude for a QOZB to utilize these exceptions by creating a working capital safe harbor.[376] Under this rule, a QOZB may hold cash, cash equivalents or debt instruments with a term of 18 months or less for 31 months (following the receipt of funds) without having such financial assets cause the QOZB to fail the asset testing requirements (and may avail itself of a second 31-month period, for a maximum of 62 months). Moreover, during the working capital safe harbor period, an entity is deemed to meet the 70-pecent tangible property standard. A QOZB satisfies the working capital safe harbor if the following conditions are satisfied:

(A) these amount (of working capital assets) are designated in writing for the development of a trade or business in a QOZ, including when appropriate the acquisition, construction and/or substantial improvement of tangible property in such zone;[377]

(B) there is a written schedule consistent with the ordinary start-up of a trade or business for the expenditure of the working capital assets. Under the schedule, the working capital assets must be spent within 31 months of the receipt by the business of such assets;[378]

(C) the working capital assets are actually used in a manner that is substantially consistent with the first two requirements listed above. However, if consumption of the working capital assets is delayed by waiting for governmental action the application or which is complete, the delay does not cause a failure under this paragraph;[379] and

(D) If the QOZB is located in a QOZ within a federally declared disaster zone (as defined under §165(i)(5)(A)), the QOZB may receive an additional 24 months to consume its working capital assets (so long as each application independently meets the requirements of Reg. §1.1400Z2(d)-1(d)(3)(v)(A)-(C).

(E) a business may benefit from multiple overlapping or sequential applications of the working capital safe harbor (provided that each allocation independently satisfies all of the requirements of sections (A)-(C) above).[380]

The Regulations permit a QOZB that is a start-up business to benefit from one or more 31-month periods, for a total of 62 months (in the form of multiple overlapping safe harbors) if the following requirements are met:[381]

1. Each application independently satisfies the requirements of Reg. §1.1400Z2(d)-1(d)(3)(v)(A)-(C).

2. The working capital assets form the expiring 31-month period were expended with the requirements of Reg. §1.1400Z2(d)-1(d)(3)(v)(A)-(C).

3. The subsequent infusions of working capital assets form an integral part of the plan covered by the initial working capital safe harbor period; and

4. Each overlapping of sequential application of the working capital safe harbor includes a substantial amount of working capital assets.

The working capital safe harbor applies only to a QOZB (and not directly to a QOF that hold QOZBP). From a planning perspective, a QOZB may meet the working capital safe harbor if it holds debt instruments with a term of 18 months or less (and the income with respect to such loans is considered "good" income under the active trade or business rules). **A QOZB that receives excess contributions or financing proceeds can therefore utilize such funds (including loaning them to related parties).**

The Regulations provided an example where a partnership placed qualified funds in working capital, where it remained until used. The partnership had written plans to acquire land in a QOZ on which it planned to construct a commercial building. The written plans provided for the purchase of land within a month of receipt and a portion allocated to the construction of the building and other necessary expenses to be spent within the next 30 months. All expenditures were made on schedule. During the 31-month period, the Partnership had no gross income other than derived from the working capital. In its analysis, the partnership met all three requirements of the working safe harbor and the expenditures are deemed reasonable as there was a written plan consistent with a startup and the funds were used within 31 months as provided for in the written plan. [382]

Importantly, the Regulations provide certain safe harbors to avoid causing entities that utilize the working capital safe harbor to fail other criteria under the opportunity zone program.

| Requirement | Safe Harbor |
|---|---|
| 50-percent Gross Income Test | Any gross income derived from working capital assets that are subject to a working capital safe harbor are counted toward the satisfaction of the test.[383] |
| Intangible Property Test | Intangible property purchased or licensed by the trade or business pursuant to a valid working capital safe harbor satisfies the use requirement.[384] |
| Non Qualified Financial Property | Working capital assets are treated as reasonable as long as the requirements of the working |

| | capital safe harbor are met.[385] |
|---|---|
| 70-percent Tangible Property Test | While the working capital safe harbor is in effect, the entity meets the 70-percent tangible property standard.[386] |

For the purposes of satisfying the incorporated §1397(c) requirements, in a case where real property straddles a QOZ, a QOZ is the location of services, tangible property or business function if (i) the trade or business uses the portion of the real property located within a QOZ in carrying out its business activities; (ii) the trade or business uses the portion of the real property located outside a QOZ in carrying out its business activities; (iii) the amount of the real property located within the QOZ is substantial compared to the property outside the QOZ; and (iv) the real property is contiguous to at least a part of the real property outside the QOZ.[387] Substantiality is determined by whether is real property in the QOZ is greater than real property outside the QOZ based on square footage or unadjusted cost.[388]

The Regulations provide significant guidance for purchasing, constructing and rehabilitating real estate. However, it may provide compliance challenges for operating businesses such as retailers, financial institutions, consultants and other operating business. These challenges and the required benchmarks need to be addressed in the planning stages of setting up a QOZB.

## CERTAIN ACTIVITIES ARE PROHIBITED (NO "SIN" BUSINESSES)

The fifth requirement of the rule applicable to a QOZB is that certain activities will not qualify as a QOZB. Specifically, a QOZB may not engage in the trade or business of (including the provision of land for) any private or commercial golf course, country club, massage parlor, hot tub facility, suntan facility, racetrack or other facility used for gambling, or any store the principal business of which is the sale of alcoholic beverages for consumption off premises.[389] The final Regulations included a de minimis exception allowing a QOZB to derive gross income not exceeding 5-percent from a "sin" business.[390] While not specifically enumerated in §144 as a "sin business", Treasury Secretary Steven Mnuchin advised against marijuana businesses claiming benefits under §1400Z-2, even if they are legal at the state level.[391] Nevertheless, no such explicit restriction was included in the Regulations.

While a QOZB may not be a "sin" business, under the available statutory and regulatory guidance, there is no such prohibition of a QOF investing in, or conducting, a "sin business". While it is unclear as to the regulatory intent, it appears that as long as QOF meets the 90-percent holding test, it could potentially invest or participate in a "sin" business.

# CHAPTER ELEVEN

# Anti-Abuse Rules

The rules of §1400Z must be applied in a manner consisted with the purposes of the opportunity zone rules. The operative statute provides that "the Secretary shall prescribe such regulations as may be necessary or appropriate to carry out the purposes of this section, including . . . rules to prevent abuse."[392] If Treasury determines that the purpose of a transaction is inconsistent with §14000-Z, it can recast a transaction as appropriate to achieve tax results consistent with the QOZ program.[393] Whether a tax result is inconsistent must be determined based on all the facts and circumstances.[394]

Treasury's enumerated purpose of the OZ program is to "provide specified Federal income tax benefits to owners of QOFs to encourage the making of longer-term investments, through QOFs and qualified opportunity zone businesses, of new capital in one or more qualified opportunity zones and to increase the economic growth of such qualified opportunity zones."[395]

The Treasury Regulations provide several examples discussing the anti-abuse rules:

1) Non-resident aliens are not subject to tax on capital gain transactions. Thus, the non-resident aliens create a domestic partnership funded by an asset intended to generate a capital gain, which would be reinvested in a QOF. Since the partnership was forced to avoid OZ requirements, the partnership is disregarded for purposes of deferring the gain.[396]

2) A QOZB purchases land in QOZ without a plan or intent to develop or use the land in a trade or business that would increase substantially the economic productivity of the land. Instead, the QOZB paves the land to create a parking lot. On the land, the QOZB will install a gate, a small office for the parking attendant, and two self-pay stations. The QOZB does not plan to expand the lot or increase the number of employees. Because the purpose in acquiring the land was to sell the land at a profit, it is inconsistent with the purposes of the OZ rules. The land is not QOZBP and the gain from sale of land will not be excluded under the opportunity zone rules.[397]

On the other hand, if the land is used in an active trade or business and significant investment are made in capital improvements to the land, the land would not be considered to be held purely for speculative investment and consistent with §1400Z-2.[398] The difference lies in the intent of the QOZB to more than substantially improve the land.

3) Taxpayer sell stock at a capital gain and invest in QOF, which in turn invest in a QOZB. The QOZB uses the investment to purchase gold, rent a safe deposit box and hire one employee to manage the purchase and sale of the gold bars. The QOZB purchases additional gold bars and sell to customers a portion of the gold bars each year. At commencement, the QOZB does not expect the business or number of employees to increase. It does believe that the gold will appreciate in value.

The gold bar business is speculative and is not expected to increase economic activity in the opportunity zone. The gold bars are not QOZBP and the QOZB would fail unless it owns or leases other assets that are QOZBP.[399]

In order to make sure that the investment qualifies, the intent behind the OZ rules should be evaluated and compared to the goal of the investment.

If a QOF fails to meet the 90-percent requirement, the QOF shall pay a penalty for each month it fails to meet the requirement.[400] The penalty is calculated based on the excess of (i) amount equal to 90-percent of its aggregate assets over (ii) the aggregate amount of QOZP held by the QOF multiplied by the underpayment established under §6621(a)(2).[401] The underpayment rate is the sum of the federal short term rate plus 3-percent. [402] For a partnership, the penalty shall be taken into account proportionally as part of the distributive share of each partner.[403]

One item of note is that the QOF does not have to meet the 90-percent test on each testing date, rather the QOF is required to hold at least 90-percent of its asset based on the average of the percentage of QOZP held on the two testing dates.

The penalty will not be imposed when the failure to meet the 90-percent requirement is based on reasonable cause.[404] While the Regulations to not expand on the language or define what is reasonable cause, the general standard is based on whether a taxpayer exercised ordinary business prudence based on the available facts and circumstance.

In a situation where a QOF failed to meet the test as a result of a lower tier entity failing to meet the requirements for a QOZB, they could still meet the test as long as the QOZB failure is corrected within 6 month of the date on which the stock or partnership lost its qualification.[405] In such a circumstance, a QOF is permitted only one correction.[406]

# CHAPTER TWELVE

# State Taxation

In general, state income taxes (with respect to states that impose income taxes) follow federal tax rules as set forth under the Code, except as modified by state income tax statutes. Majority of the states recognize the federal tax benefits of the OZ program. Some states created restrictions by limiting the benefits to in-state investments. Others have embraced the program and incentivized such investments with credits and other benefits.

Whether a state follows the Internal Revenue Code is dependent on its conformity date. Eighteen states, as well as the District of Columbia, automatically conform to new federal tax laws. Nineteen states must update their fixed-date conformity statutes in order to adopt the new provisions. All other states either have no tax or conform selectively as set forth in the following table.

| State | Individual | Corporate |
| --- | --- | --- |
| Alabama | Partially Conforming | Partially Conforming |

| | | |
|---|---|---|
| **Alaska** | No Capital Gains Tax | Conforming |
| **Arizona** | Conforming | Conforming |
| **Arkansas** | **Partially Conforming** | **Partially Conforming** |
| **California** | **Nonconforming** | **Nonconforming** |
| **Colorado** | Conforming | Conforming |
| **Connecticut** | Conforming | Conforming |
| **Delaware** | Conforming | Conforming |
| **District of Columbia** | Conforming | Conforming |
| **Florida** | No Capital Gains Tax | Conforming |
| **Georgia** | Conforming | Conforming |
| **Hawaii** | **Partially Conforming** | Partially Conforming |
| **Idaho** | Conforming | Conforming |
| **Illinois** | Conforming | Conforming |
| **Indiana** | Conforming | Conforming |
| **Iowa** | Conforming | Conforming |
| **Kansas** | Conforming | Conforming |
| **Kentucky** | Conforming | Conforming |
| **Louisiana** | Conforming | Conforming |
| **Maine** | Conforming | Conforming |
| **Maryland** | Conforming | Conforming |
| **Massachusetts** | **Nonconforming** | Conforming |
| **Michigan** | Conforming | Conforming |
| **Minnesota** | Conforming | Conforming |
| **Mississippi** | **Nonconforming** | **Nonconforming** |
| **Missouri** | Conforming | Conforming |
| **Montana** | Conforming | Conforming |
| **Nebraska** | Conforming | Conforming |
| **Nevada** | No Capital Gains Tax | No Capital Gains Tax |
| **New Hampshire** | No Capital Gains Tax | **Nonconforming** |

| | | |
|---|---|---|
| **New Jersey** | Conforming | Conforming |
| **New Mexico** | Conforming | Conforming |
| **New York** | **Partially Conforming** | **Partially Conforming** |
| **North Carolina** | **Nonconforming** | **Nonconforming** |
| **North Dakota** | Conforming | Conforming |
| **Ohio** | Conforming | No Capital Gains Tax |
| **Oklahoma** | Conforming | Conforming |
| **Oregon** | Conforming | Conforming |
| **Pennsylvania** | Conforming | **Nonconforming** |
| **Rhode Island** | Conforming | Conforming |
| **South Carolina** | Conforming | Conforming |
| **South Dakota** | No Capital Gains Tax | No Capital Gains Tax |
| **Tennessee** | No Capital Gains Tax | Conforming |
| **Texas** | No Capital Gains Tax | No Capital Gains Tax |
| **Utah** | Conforming | Conforming |
| **Vermont** | Conforming | Conforming |
| **Virginia** | Conforming | Conforming |
| **Washington** | No Capital Gains Tax | No Capital Gains Tax |
| **West Virginia** | Conforming | Conforming |
| **Wisconsin** | Conforming | Conforming |
| **Wyoming** | No Capital Gains Tax | No Capital Gains Tax |

Some of the distinctions for the non-conforming states are as follows:

- Arkansas limits opportunity zone benefits to investments located in its respective state.
- California does not recognize OZ benefits.
- Hawaii permits OZ benefits to opportunity zone within its state as designated by its governor.

- Massachusetts does not recognize the OZ benefits under its personal income tax rules. However, it does conform for deferrals and investments claimed by corporations.
- New York recently passed a state budge with provisions to decouple its capital gain treatment from the federal Opportunity Zone program. However, it will still follow the federal treatment that appreciated investment after a 10-year holding are nontaxable.

QOZ designations may overlap with local, state and federal programs that were passed to promote investments in economically distressed communities. The Ohio General Assembly approved an income tax credit for Ohio based investment in opportunity zone. Wisconsin allows an income subtraction and an additional capital gain exclusion (or basis adjustment) for investments in an in-state qualified opportunity fund.

In order to promote the tax benefits of the QOZ, several states have complementary programs that work either independently or in conjunction with federal requirements. Potentially, a single QOF transaction could involve multiple jurisdictions. This could result in a necessary state apportionment of the capital gains and/or differing recognition periods. Taxpayers seeking QOZ investment opportunities should consider available local, state and other federal incentives. Based on the investment, a review of each specific state's regulations, complimentary programs and tax effects should be considered before setting up an investment vehicle.

# CHAPTER THIRTEEN

# Coordination with Other Credits and Incentives

A QOF (or QOZB) may qualify for federal tax credits in addition to the tax incentives available under the QOZ program. Indeed, it is likely that many (if not most) QOFs will be eligible for additional credits under complementary tax credit programs including the New Markets Tax Credit ("NMTC"),[407] federal historic rehabilitation tax credit,[408] or low income housing tax credit ("LIHTC").[409] Likewise, the development activities of a QOF (which may be infrastructure, energy or operating business related) may also permit credits for research and development,[410] energy property (which may consist of solar, wind, geothermal and renewable energy sources),[411] and workforce development.[412]

The NMTC is the most obvious complement to the QOZ program. The NMTC provides tax credits for certain investments in low-income communities. Since QOZs are, by definition, a "low-income community" as defined in §45D(e) (or an adjacent parcel that meets certain criteria),[413] nearly all QOZs will be located in geographic areas eligible for the NMTC. The vehicle utilized for purposes of obtaining credits under the NMTC program is the use of a "qualified community development entity" ("QCDE").[414]

QOZs that intend to utilize NMTCs may face stiff competition to obtain the credits in in the coming years. The NMTC program has an annual limit of $3.5 billion (as of 2019) of NMTCs allocated by Treasury's Community Development Financial Institution's Fund. Since almost all QOFs may qualify under the NMTC program, and the QOZ program will spur extensive new development in low-income communities, the $3.5 billion allocation may be insufficient in light of the increase in projects.

A QOF may qualify as a QCDE, which generally would allow an investor to generate tax credits equal to 39-percent the investment by an investor into a QDCE. Such credits are generated over six years (in seven installments).[415] In order to structure a QCDE that will qualify as a QOF, the QCDE would likely make an equity investment into an active trade or business activity in a low-income community.[416]

Under the NMTC program, the minimum investment period is typically seven years. This period may run concurrently with the 10-year period for an investor to hold its QOF investment and obtain tax-free capital gains at disposition.

Treasury has issued guidance to address the coordination of the rules under the NMTC program and the QOZ program. For example, the working capital safe harbor for a QOZB allows for a 31-month period in which financial assets will not cause penalties or disqualification; the NMTC program only permits 12 months for a similar purpose. Likewise, under §45D(h), the issuance of a credit under the NMTC program to an investor causes a reduction in the investor's basis. If the investor has no basis (since an investor's basis in a QOF is zero, until the basis is subsequently adjusted), the credit may either cause taxable gain or could be at-risk (alternatively, the credit would be allowed if the investor has sufficient debt basis at the time that the credit allocated to the investor).

The LIHTC program may also be coordinated with a QOF investment. Under the LIHTC program, an investor is able to obtain tax credits over a 10-year period with respect to the construction of low-income housing projects.[417] The credits under the LIHTC program are allocated by state agencies in exchange for a building providing low-income housing for 15 or 30 years. Although the qualification under the LIHT program is outside the scope of this discussion, a low-income housing development project (that meets the substantial improvement test) and is located in a QOZ could generate substantial additional tax benefits to an investor.[418]

For certain specific projects, the historic rehabilitation tax credit may also be utilized in conjunction with a QOF investment. Similar the QOZ program, the historic rehabilitation credit requires that the basis of the building be doubled over a 24 month period.[419] The credit is allowed over a five year period that may run concurrent with an investor's holding period of a QOF.[420] As with the other credit programs, the basis rules under §47 will need to be reconciled with the basis rules under §1400Z-2 (so that required basis reductions can be properly reflected).

Outside of real estate, §1202 provides for tax-free gains from the disposition of qualified small business stock ("QSBS") after a 5 year holding period.[421] QSBS must be stock in a C corporation that conducts an active trade or business (and meets certain other requirements). Since a QOF or a QOZB may be a C corporation, such entity could qualify for both incentives. The primary advantage of using QSBS is that the holding period to obtain tax-free gains is only 5 years.[422] The QOF program allows for potential for unlimited tax-free appreciation and does not contain restrictions on the amount of business assets. Thus, the §1202 incentives can, in effect, provide a hedge for early stage businesses that could monetize in a shorter time frame than is provided for under the QOZ program.

# Appendices

## The ABCs Of OZs (A Glossary of Key Terms And Abbreviations)

"**Eligible Interest**" generally refers to an equity interest issued by the QOF, including preferred stock or partnership interest with special allocations.[423]

"**Eligible Taxpayer**" is a person that is required to report the recognition of gains during the taxable year under Federal income tax accounting principles..[424]

"**Inclusion event**" means an event described in paragraph (c) of Reg. §1.1400Z2(b)-1, reflecting the circumstances in which deferred gain is included in income.[425]

"**Mixed-funds investment**" means an investment a portion of which is a qualifying investment and a portion of which is a non-qualifying investment.[426]

"**Non-qualifying investment**" means an investment in a QOF described in §1400Z-2(e)(1)(A)(ii) (relating to the treatment of an investment with mixed funds).[427]

"**QOF**" or "**qualified opportunity fund**" means any investment vehicle that is organized as a partnership or corporation (for the purpose of investing in qualified opportunity zone property) that holds at least 90 percent of its assets in QOZP.[428]

"**QOF corporation**" means a QOF that is classified as a corporation for Federal income tax purposes.[429]

"**QOF C corporation**" means a QOF corporation other than a QOF S corporation.[430]

"**QOF owner**" means a QOF shareholder or a QOF partner.[431]

"**QOF S corporation**" means a QOF corporation that has elected under §1362 to be an S corporation.[432]

"**QOF shareholder**" means a person that directly owns a qualifying investment in a QOF corporation.[433]

"**QOZB**" or "**qualified opportunity zone business**" means a trade or business (i) in which substantially all of the tangible property owned or leased by the taxpayer is qualified opportunity zone business property (determined by substituting "qualified opportunity zone business" for "qualified opportunity fund" each place it appears in paragraph (2)(D)), (ii) which satisfies the requirements of paragraphs (2), (4), and (8) of section 1397C(b), and (iii) which is not described in section 144(c)(6)(B).

"**QOZBP**" or "**qualified opportunity zone business property**" means tangible property used in a trade or business of the qualified opportunity fund if (I) such property was acquired by the qualified opportunity fund by purchase (as defined in §179(d)(2)) after December 31, 2017, (II) the original use of such property in the qualified opportunity zone commences with the qualified opportunity fund or the qualified opportunity fund substantially improves the property, and (III) during substantially all of the qualified opportunity fund's holding period for such property, substantially all of the use of such property was in a qualified opportunity zone.[434]

"**QOZ Partnership**" or "**qualified opportunity zone partnership interest**" means any capital or profits interest in a domestic partnership if (i) such interest is acquired by the qualified opportunity fund after December 31, 2017, from the partnership solely in exchange for cash, (ii) as of the time such interest was acquired, such partnership was a qualified opportunity zone business (or, in the case of a new partnership, such partnership was being organized for purposes of being a qualified opportunity zone business), and (iii) during substantially all of the qualified opportunity fund's holding period for such interest, such partnership qualified as a qualified opportunity zone business.[435]

"**QOZP**" or "**qualified opportunity zone property**" means property which is (i) qualified opportunity zone stock, (ii) qualified opportunity zone partnership interest, or (iii) qualified opportunity zone business property.[436]

"**QOZ Stock**" or "**qualified opportunity zone stock**" means any stock in a domestic corporation if (I) such stock is acquired by the qualified opportunity fund after December 31, 2017, at its original issue (directly or through an underwriter) from the corporation solely in exchange for cash, (II) as of the time such stock was issued, such corporation was a qualified opportunity zone business (or, in the case of a new corporation, such corporation was being organized for purposes of being a qualified opportunity zone business), and (III) during substantially all of the qualified opportunity fund's holding period for such stock, such corporation qualified as a qualified opportunity zone business.[437]

"**Qualifying investment**" means an eligible interest (as defined in §1.1400Z2(a)-1(b)(3)), or portion thereof, in a QOF to the extent that a deferral election applies with respect to such eligible interest or portion thereof.[438]

"**Remaining deferred gain**" means the full amount of gain that was deferred under §1400Z-2(a)(1)(A), reduced by the amount of gain previously included as a result of an inclusion event.

"**Working Capital Safe Harbor**" is not an explicitly defined term, but refers to the working capital safe harbor described in Reg. §1.1400Z2(d)-1(d)(5)(iv) that provides that for a period of 31 months, a QOZB will fail to meet the asset holding tests if it holds qualifying financial property (i.e., cash, cash equivalents or debt instruments with a term of 18 months or less) that will be used (pursuant to a written plan) to acquire, construct or develop QOZBP.

# TIMELINE OF A QOF INVESTMENT

| | |
|---|---|
| **JULY 1, 2019** | Taxpayer reinvests $10 Million of capital gains into a QOF. The QOF contributes the cash to a newly formed QOZB. |
| **JUL. 2, 2019** | QOZB acquires land and building for $30 million with $10M of cash and $20M from a new construction loan. This commences the working capital safe harbor period. |
| **JUL. 2, 2019** | Working capital safe harbor period (31 months) ⟶ **Dec. 31, 2021**<br>Substantial improvement period (30 months) |
| **JAN. 1, 2020** | QOF will self-certify as a QOF by filing Form 8996 (3/15). ⟶ **Dec. 31, 2021**<br>Taxpayer will defer capital gains (Form 8949 and 8997) (4/15) |
| **JUL. 1, 2024/6** | Investor's basis is increased by $1 million on July 1, 2024 (5 year holding period) and by another $500,000 on July 1, 2026 (7 year holding period) |
| **DEC 31, 2026** | Investor recognizes $8.5 million of capital gains, or less if the fair market value of the interest has declined in value |
| **JULY 3, 2029** | QOZB sells property, resulting in gain to QOF which, in turn, makes the asset sale election to exclude gain. Alternatively, the Investor sells QOF interest directly. |
| **TAX SEASON 2030** | The QOF (or the Investor) excludes the gain by applying the rules and Regulations under Section 1400Z-2(c) and filing all appropriate tax returns and forms consistent with IRS requirements. |

## Sample Structure

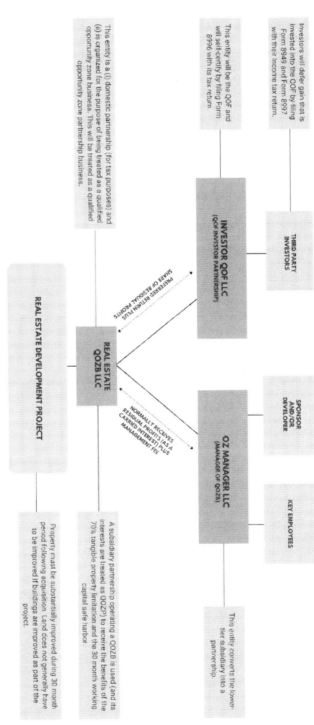

Investors will defer gain that is invested into the QOF by filing Form 8949 and Form 8997 with their income tax return.

This entity will be the QOF and will self-certify by filing Form 8996 with its tax return.

This entity is a (i) domestic partnership (for tax purposes) and (ii) is organized for the purpose of being treated as a qualified opportunity zone business. This will be treated as a qualified opportunity zone partnership business.

THIRD PARTY INVESTORS

INVESTOR QOF LLC
(QOF INVESTOR PARTNERSHIP)

SPONSOR AND/OR DEVELOPER

REAL ESTATE QOZB LLC

OZ MANAGER LLC
(MANAGER OF QOZB)

KEY EMPLOYEES

PREFERRED RETURN PLUS
SHARE OF RESIDUAL PROFITS

NORMALLY RECEIVES
RESIDUAL PROFITS (AS A
CARRIED INTEREST) PLUS
MANAGEMENT FEE

REAL ESTATE DEVELOPMENT PROJECT

A subsidiary partnership operating a QOZB is used (and its interests are treated as QOZP) to receive the benefits of the 70% tangible property limitation and the 30 month working capital safe harbor.

Property must be substantially improved during 30 month period following acquisition. Land does not generally have to be improved if buildings are improved as part of the project.

This entity converts the lower-tier subsidiary into a partnership.

## *About RS&F*

Rosen, Sapperstein & Friedlander, LLC (RS&F) is the leading firm in the Mid-Atlantic region that provides business consulting and accounting services that cater to middle-market businesses, ultra-high net worth families, and family offices. Our team is comprised of outstanding professionals who service clients with passion, focus, and entrepreneurial spirit. As a full-service CPA firm, RS&F provides consulting, tax, audit, forensic accounting, business valuation, and accounting services. The Firm works with clients in a variety of industries, including real estate, construction, healthcare, nonprofits, government contractors, business services, manufacturers, distributors, automotive, technology, and mortgage lending.

RS&F has offices in Towson and Columbia, Maryland.

**Mission**

We are on a journey with our team, clients, and community as trusted partners, helping them thrive, supporting their success, and making sustainable impact. Together, we care, we grow, and we achieve!

**Vision**

RS&F approaches business as entrepreneurs and this mindset permeates through our client relationships, service delivery, and outstanding team. Our clients deserve sophisticated guidance to help them make effective decisions affecting their businesses, family, and community. Values such as quality, integrity, independence, and accessibility are important, but can be used to describe most professional service firms. RS&F is atypical and our clients benefit from our teams' clarity, creativity, focus, humility, and persistence. The pace of change in today's world requires our clients to rapidly evolve and partner with a team of advisors who are committed to their success.

## BDO Alliance

RS&F is a member of the BDO Alliance. The association is comprised of approximately 285 highly successful independent public accounting firms with over 700 locations in the United States. The BDO Alliance provides its independent member firms with tools and resources to help them furnish superior accounting, auditing, tax and management services to clients around the globe including direct access to the resources of BDO, the 5th largest accounting firm in the world. Through BDO Alliance, independent member firms offer the strength and capabilities of a large, worldwide organization with technical depth and geographic reach impossible for a local firm alone. RS&F frequently leverages the deep knowledge of our peers at BDO and member firms in the BDO Alliance to benefit clients and their capabilities provide significant depth to our client service offerings. Additional information regarding the BDO Alliance can be found at https://www.bdo.com/about/bdo-alliance-usa.

ENDNOTES

# Notes and Citations

[1] Section 1400Z-1 and §1400Z-2 of the Internal Revenue Code of 1986, as amended ("Code"). All Section references contained herein refer to such section of the Code or the Treasury Regulations promulgated thereunder. This program is sometimes referred to as the "qualified opportunity zone legislation" or "QOZ legislation".

[2] The House version of the Investing in Opportunity Act was sponsored by Rep. Patrick Tiberi (R) and cosponsored by 81 representatives comprised of 45 Republicans and 36 Democrats. The Senate version was sponsored by Senator Tim Scott and cosponsored by 14 Senators comprised of 7 Republicans and 7 Democrats.

[3] The referenced white paper issued by EIG was authored by Jared Bernstein of the Center on Budget and Policy Priorities and Kevin A. Bassett of the American Enterprise Institute. EIG describes itself as "a bipartisan public policy organization that combines innovative research and data-driven advocacy to address America's most pressing economic challenges."

[4] https://www.forbes.com/sites/jenniferpryce/2018/08/14/theres-a-6-trillion-opportunity-in-opportunity-zones-heres-what-we-need-to-do-to-make-good-on-it/#7a26fb006ffc

[5] https://eig.org/opportunityzones/history

[6] https://fas.org/sgp/crs/misc/R45152.pdf

[7] Notice 2018-48; Notice 2019-42 and Announcement 2021-10.

[8] This rule makes December 31, 2026 the last day that any deferred capital gains would be recognized (and the last day that any gains could be invested in a QOF would therefore be June 28, 2027). For many taxpayers, this recognition date would effectively defer payment of the tax until April 15, 2027 (subject to estimated tax liabilities).

[9] Such interests will be considered a QOZB if (1) at least 70-percent of its property is considered QOZBP; (2) 50% of the gross income is derived from the active conduct of the trade or business; (3) at least 40% of the intangible property of the business is used in the active conduct of the trade or business; (4) no more than 5% of the property of the QOZB consists of financial property (*e.g.*, cash and investments); and (5) the trades or businesses are not comprised of "sin" businesses.

[10] If the underlying property as sold, the Investors would instead elect to exclude the K-1 income. If such election is made, some of the gain may not be eliminated due to limitations inherent in the asset sale exclusion election (which are described in much more detail in Part 5).

[11] In our example we use a $100 million investment. The same math will apply whether the investment size is $1 million or $100 billion and the use of $100 million is merely to illustrate the effect with respect to a project under the QOZ program.

[12] We typically use a 65% loan to value (LTV) as a baseline for a construction loan. To keep the math as simple as possible, we have kept the nominal amounts 'simple" (which results in a 67% LTV), which is close enough to the baseline for illustration purposes.

[13] For any other inclusion event, the amount of gain that an investor will include in income (as of the respective inclusion date) is the proportionate amount of the remaining deferred gain based on the fair market value of the investment that was deemed to be sold.

[14] Note that for venture funds that generate substantial tax-free gains under §1202 for dispositions of qualified small business stock, the increased IRR from a QOZ will be reduced substantially since §1202 gains are already tax-free in whole or in part.

[15] This statement is not intended to reflect that a real estate seller can easily obtain the actual fair market value of a real estate holding. However, it is not difficult to find a potential buyer of raw land or vacant buildings (although the price offered may be far less than the seller's expectations) while finding a buyer for any operating business is a much more arduous task. The market for revenue generating real estate is extremely active – and therefore one can obtain market prices.

[16] If the founder contributed, rather than sold, nonqualified assets to the QOF, it would likely result in a mixed funds investment for the owner and could cause the QOF to fail the asset qualification tests.

[17] See §45D.

[18] Notice 2018-48; Notice 2019-42 (adding two additional census tracts in Puerto Rico) and Announcement 2021-10 (confirming that the census tracts that have been designated are final and not subject to change and are properly based on the 2010 census and such tracts will not be modified based on the 2020 census).

[19] On January 13, 2020, Treasury issued the final regulations (the "Regulations") with respect to §1400Z-2, replacing the Proposed Regulations issued on October 19, 2018 (the "2018 Proposed Regulations") and April 17, 2019 (the "2019 Proposed Regulations" and, together with the 2018 Proposed Regulations, the "Proposed Regulations").

[20] §1400Z-2(a)(1) and §1400Z-2(b).

[21] §1400Z-2(b)(2)(B)(iii).

[22] Since the remaining deferred gain would be recognized in income as provided under §1400Z-2(b) on December 31, 2026, the five-year holding period would not be met prior to gain inclusion, thus preventing the step up from applying to any investments made after that date.

[23] §1400Z-2(b)(2)(B)(iv).

[24] Since the remaining deferred gain would be recognized in income as provided under §1400Z-2(b) on December 31, 2026, the seven-year holding period would not be met prior to gain inclusion, thus preventing the step up from applying to any investments made after that date.

[25] §1400Z-2(c).

[26] §1400Z-2(b)(2)(A)(i).

[27] Part 3, C. contains a brief economic analysis and sample IRR calculation.

[28] §1400Z-2(a)(1)(B) provides that the amount of gain excluded (as provided in the previous paragraph) will be *included* as provided in Section 1400Z-2(b) (in accordance with the "inclusion rules" discussed below). §1400Z-2(a)(1)(C) explicitly provides that the tax-free gain applicable to investments held over ten years will apply to a qualifying investment.

[29] Reg. §1.1400Z2(a)-1(b)(11).

[30] A technical question arises as to whether a taxpayer may opt out of installment sale treatment for a post-2026 gain under §453(d) followed by a deferral of gain through reinvestment in a QOF. Since the taxpayer would only opt-out because it is eligible to defer under §1400Z-2, arguably this provision could cause inclusion for post 2026 gains.

[31] Reg. §1.1400Z2(a)-1(b)(11)(i).

[32] Reg. §1.1400Z2(a)-1(b)(11)(i)(A)(1).

[33] Reg. §1.1400Z2(a)-1(b)(11)(i)(A)(2).

[34] Reg. §1.1400Z2(a)-1(b)(11)(ii).

[35] Reg. §1.1400Z2(a)-1(b)(11)(iv).

[36] *See* Preamble to the 2018 Proposed Regulations.

[37] Note the distinction between "unrecaptured §1250 gain" which is capital gain taxed at a higher rate as opposed to §1250 depreciation recapture, which is taxed at ordinary rates. Only the unrecaptured §1250 gain that is treated as capital gain is eligible for reinvestment.

[38] §1(h).

[39] §1231(c)(3) (defining "net section 1231 gain").

[40] https://www.irs.gov/newsroom/opportunity-zones-frequently-asked-questions

[41] Reg. §1.1400Z2(a)-1(b)(11)(vi).

[42] Reg. §1.1400Z2(a)-1(b)(11)(vi)(B).

[43] Reg. §1.1400Z2(a)-1(b)(11)(vi)(C).

[44] Reg. §1.1400Z2(a)-1(b)(11)(v).

[45] Reg. §1.1400Z2(a)-1(c)(1).

[46] Reg. §1.1400Z2(a)-1(c)(1)(ii).

[47] Reg. §1.1400Z2(a)-1(c)(1)(iii).

[48] Reg. §1.1400Z2(a)-1(c)(1)(iii)(B).

[49] Reg. §1.1400Z2(a)-1(c)(1)(iii)(C).

[50] Reg. §1.1400Z2(a)-1(c)(2).

[51] Reg. §1.1400Z2(a)-1(c)(3).

[52] Note that while this approach will work for portfolio capital gains (which is based on a taxpayer's residence), it may not apply to capital gains resulting from the sale of assets that are specifically apportioned to a state. In other words, where the gain is capital gain because of a business nexus to that state (as compared to whether state taxation arises solely due to the taxpayer's residence) then such state tax may still apply.

[53] In order to determine the economic impact of such a strategy, we recommend analyzing the tax consequences on a present value basis.

[54] Note that gain resulting from certain types of dispositions, such as corporate and partnership liquidations, may be considered a gain from a related party and ineligible for deferral under §1400Z-2.

[55] *Helvering v. William Flaccus Oak Leather Co.*, 313 U.S. 247 (1941).

[56] *Grodt & McKay Realty, Inc. v. Commissioner*, 77 T.C. 1221 (1981).

[57] See *Nahey v. Commissioner*, 111 T.C. 256 (1998), aff'd on other grounds, 196 F.3d 866 (7th Cir. 1999), cert. denied, 121 S. Ct. 45 (2000).

[58] *Grodt & McKay Realty, Inc. v. Commissioner*, 77 T.C. 1221 (1981).

[59] *Rogers v. Commissioner*, 103 F.2d 790 (9th Cir. 1939); Guardian Indus. Corp. v. Commissioner, 97 T.C. 308 (1991).

[60] *Derr v. Commissioner*, 77 T.C. 708, 724 (1981).

[61] See *United States v. Ivey*, 414 F.2d 199 (5th Cir. 1969); *Guardian Indus. Corp. v. Commissioner*, 97 T.C. 308, 308 fn. 5 (1991).

[62] *Helvering v. William Flaccus Oak Leather Co.*, 313 U.S. 247 (1941).

[63] *Cottage Savings Ass'n v. Commissioner*, 499 U.S. 554 (1991).

[64] See Reg. §1.1001-3. See also Rev. Proc. 2001-21, 2001-9 I.R.B. 742 (election to treat a substitution of DIs in certain circumstances as a realization event even though it does not result in a significant modification).

[65] Note that taxpayers often prefer to treat income resulting from a debt workout or restructuring as cancellation of indebtedness ("COD") income under §108. First, COD income may be excluded under §108(a)(1) for a taxpayer that is bankrupt, insolvent (up the amount of insolvency) or for qualified real property business indebtedness. To the extent that income is excluded under these rules, the taxpayer will have to reduce various tax attributes (*e.g.*, basis in depreciable property or net operating losses). The ability to reinvest gains in a QOF resulting from a material modification (if not characterized as COD income) may be a solution for taxpayers that cannot benefit from the exclusions under the COD rules.

[66] Reg. §1.1400Z2(a)-1(b)(11)(i)(C).

[67] 1400Z-2(e)(2). Reg. §1.1400Z2(a)-1(b)(39).

[68] §267(b).

[69] §267(c).

[70] §267(c)(4).

[71] Reg. §1.1400Z2(a)-1(a)(2) & §1.1400Z(a)-1(d)(1).

[72] https://www.irs.gov/pub/irs-pdf/f8997.pdf

[73] Reg. §1.1400Z2(a)-1(d)(2).

[74] Reg. §1.1400Z2(a)-1(b)(13) . A tax-exempt entity subject to tax under §511, the unrelated business income tax rules, is permitted to make a QOF investment.

[75] Reg. §1.1400Z2(a)-1(b)(24).

[76] Reg. §1.1400Z2(a)-1(b)(12)(i).

[77] Reg. §1.1400Z2(a)-1(b)(12)(ii). Under this rule, an equity interest is explicitly permitted to be used as security for a loan.

[78] Reg. §1.1400Z2(a)-1(c)(5)(iii), Reg. §1.1400Z2(a)-1(b)(12)(i).

[79] Reg. §1.1400Z2(a)-1(c)(5)(iii).

[80] Reg. §1.1400Z2(a)-1(c)(5)(i).

[81] Such transaction constitutes an eligible investment whether or not the transferor recognized gain or loss on the property transferred.

[82] Reg. §1.1400Z2(a)-1(b)(12)(iii), §1400Z-2(a)-1(f)(2).

[83] Reg. §1.1400Z2(a)-1(c)(6).

[84] As described in §1400Z-2(e)(1)(A)(ii).

[85] Under any such structure in which there was a prearranged formula for which the debt could be converted to equity, the general debt/equity principles would be presumably apply to determine that the interest was an equity interest that may be treated as an eligible interest.

[86] Reg. §1.1400Z2(a)-1(c)(6)(ii)(A).

[87] Reg. §1.1400Z2(a)-1(c)(6)(ii)(B).

[88] Reg. §1.1400Z2(a)-1(c)(6)(ii)(B)(2).

[89] Reg. §1.1400Z2(a)-1(c)(6)(ii)(B)(3).

[90] Reg. §1.1400Z2(a)-1(c)(6)(ii)(C).

[91] A sale may not be preferable since the seller may not have cash to cover the liability when the gain is recognized (likely in 2026). Note that gain from the sale to a QOF cannot be reinvested in the QOF since it would be recharacterized as a contribution and distribution. See Reg. §1.1400Z2(f)-1(c)(3)(iii)(B) Any property acquired from a related party will be treated as non-qualifying property for purposes of the tangible property tests.

[92] See Reg. §1.1400Z2(f)-1(c)(3)(iii)(B) (example in Regulations provides that circular movement of consideration is not permitted under step transaction doctrine - circular movement of consideration is disregarded for Federal income tax purposes).

[93] §1400Z-2(e)(1). Also, as provided in Reg. §1.1400Z2(a)-1(c)(6)(ii)(D), if a taxpayer's investment is considered to be made with mixed funds under the rules of §1400Z-2(e)(1), the taxpayer's basis in the investment is equal to the taxpayer's basis in all QOF interests received, reduced by the investment to which §1400Z-2(e)(1)(A) applies (determined without regard to the basis adjustment of §1400Z-2(b)(2)(B)).

[94] Reg. §1.1400Z2(a)-1(c)(6)(iii)(A)(1).

[95] Reg. §1.1400Z2(a)-1(c)(6)(iii)(A)(2).

[96] The impact of this rule is significant. If a disguised sale is deemed to occur, not only will the investor have gain, but the original investment will also be recharacterized as a nonqualifying investment (resulting a mixed funds investment for the investor).

[97] Reg. §1.1400Z2(a)-1(c)(vi)(4).

[98] Reg. §1.1400Z2(a)-1(c)(5)(ii).

[99] The taxpayer would need to analyze any potential transaction to determine whether the distribution of cash would result in distributions in excess of basis even if no gain is allocated to the profits interest partner.

[100] §1400Z-2(a)(1)(A).

[101] Reg. §1.1400Z2(a)-1(b)(7)(iv)(A).

[102] Reg. §1.1400Z-2(a)-1(b)(7)(iv)(D).

[103] Reg. §1.1400Z-2(a)-1(b)(7)(ii)(A).

[104] Reg. §1.1400Z-2(a)-1(b)(7)(ii)(B).

[105] Reg. §1.1400Z-2(a)-1(b)(7)(ii)(B).

[106] Reg. §1.1400Z-2(a)-1(b)(7)(iv)(B).

[107] Reg. §1.1400Z-2(a)-1(b)(7)(iv)(C).

[108] Reg. §1.1400Z-2(a)-1(b)(7)(ii)(C).

[109] *See Reinvestment Rules for QOFs*, below in Section V.C.8.

[110] Reg. §1.1400Z2(a)-1(c)(8)(i).

[111] Reg. §1.1400Z2(a)-1(c)(7)(i).

[112] Reg. §1.1400Z-2(a)-1(c)(8)(ii).

[113] Reg. §1.1400Z-2(a)-1(c)(8)(iii)(A).

[114] Reg. §1.1400Z-2(a)-1(c)(8)(iii)(B).

[115] Reg. §1.1400Z2(a)-1(c)(9)(i).

[116] Reg. §1.1400Z2(a)-1(c)(9)(ii).

[117] PLR 202021009.

[118] Reg. §1.1400Z2(f)-1(b)(1).

[119] Reg. §1.1400Z2(f)-1(b)(2).

[120] Reg. §1.1400Z2(f)-1(b)(1).

[121] §1400Z-2(b)(1).

[122] Reg. §1.1400Z2(b)-1(b).

[123] Reg. §1.1400Z2(b)-1(c).

[124] Note that under Reg. §1.1400Z2(a)-1(c)(6)(iii)(A), in the case of a distribution in which the debt-financed distribution rules apply (under Reg. §1.707-5), the partner's share of the partnership liabilities is equal to zero.

[125] Reg. §1.1400Z2(b)-1(c)(1). Reg. §1.1400Z2(b)-1(c)(14) elaborates on this rule by providing that (i) the date that the taxpayer treats it investment as worthless will be the date of the inclusion event; and (ii) the rules governing basis adjustments under §1400Z-2(b)(2)(B)(iii) or §1400Z-2(c) will not apply after the date that the stock becomes worthless. We also recognize that this rule may not have any significant economic effect since the taxpayer has no basis in its qualifying QOF investment except to the extent of the 10% and 5% basis adjustments.

[126] Reg. §1.1400Z2(b)-1(c)(2)(i).

[127] Reg. §1.1400Z2(b)-1(c)(2)(i).

[128] Reg. §1.1400Z2(b)-1(c)(2)(ii).

[129] Reg. §1.1400Z2(b)-1(c)(2)(ii)(A).

[130] Reg. §1.1400Z2(b)-1(c)(2)(ii)(B). The term "QOF Owner" means either a QOF Shareholder or QOF partner. Tax free liquidations under § 332 and § 337 are not inclusion event because the 80% distribute is a successor to the QOF interest.

[131] Reg. §1.1400Z2(b)-1(d)(1)(ii)(A).

[132] Reg. §1.1400Z2(b)-1(c)(3)(i).

[133] Reg. §1.1400Z2(b)-1(c)(5)(i).

[134] A defective grantor trust is a trust that is treated as a grantor trust for income tax purposes under §§671-678 of the Code, but is not included in a decedent's estate under §2038. For example, a trust that that provides a grantor with the right to substitute trust property, but is otherwise an irrevocable trust outside of the grantor's control, will be treated as a grantor trust for income tax purposes under §675(4) but the trust assets will not be included in the grantor's estate under §2038.

[135] Reg. §1.1400Z2(b)-1(c)(4)(i).

[136] Reg. §1.1400Z2(b)-1(c)(4)(ii).

[137] Reg. §1.1400Z2(b)-1(c)(5)(ii).

[138] Reg. §1.1400Z2(b)-1(c)(5)(ii).

[139] Note that the same result will apply if the QOF interest is transferred to the defective grantor trust and the grantor remains alive until disposition. The basis step up would occur even though the asset remains outside of the transferor's estate.

[140] Reg. §1.1400Z2(b)-1(c)(6).

[141] Reg. §1.1400Z2(b)-1(c)(6)(ii)(B).

[142] Reg. §1.1400Z2(b)-1(c)(6)(ii)(C).

[143] Reg. §1.1400Z2(b)-1(c)(6)(ii)(B).

[144] §731(a)(1).

[145] Reg. §1.1400Z2(b)-1(c)(6)(iii).

[146] Reg. §1.1400Z2(a)-1(c)(6)(iii)(A)(2)

[147] Reg. §1.1400Z2(b)-1(c)(6)(iv).

[148] Reg. §1.1400Z2(b)-1(c)(6)(iv)(A). Note that it will be up to the investor to track the basis of the qualified and non-qualified portion of their investment since the QOF will not know what interests are qualified interests.

[149] Reg. §1.1400Z2(b)-1(c)(6)(iv)(B). Sensibly, the Regulations provide that §704(c) principles shall apply to account for value-basis disparities attributable to qualifying investments. Although these rules are complicated, they are well established and can be readily applies to interests in a partnership that have disproportionate differences between outside basis (of equity interests) and inside basis (of the partner's share of the partnership's basis in its assets).

[150] Reg. §1.1400Z2(b)-1(c)(6)(iv)(C).

[151] First sentence of Reg. §1.1400Z2(b)-1(c)(6)(iv)(D).

[152] Second sentence of Reg. §1.1400Z2(b)-1(c)(6)(iv)(D).

[153] Reg. §1.1400Z2(b)-1(c)(6)(v) referencing Reg. §1.1400Z2(a)-1(c)(6)(iii)(A)(2)

[154] Reg. §1.1400Z2(b)-1(c)(7)(i)(A).

[155] Reg. §1.1400Z2(b)-1(c)(7)(i)(B).

[156] Reg. §1.1400Z2(b)-1(c)(7)(i)(C).

[157] Reg. §1.1400Z2(b)-1(c)(7)(i)(D).

[158] Reg. §1.1400Z2(b)-1(c)(7)(ii).

[159] Reg. §1.1400Z2(b)-1(c)(7)(ii)(B).

[160] Reg. §1.1400Z2(b)-1(c)(7)(iv)(A).

[161] Reg. §1.1400Z2(b)-1(c)(7)(iv)(B).

[162] Reg. §1.1400Z2(b)-1(c)(9)(ii).

[163] Reg. §1.1400Z2(b)-1(c)(7)(v).

[164] Reg. §1.1400Z2(b)-1(c)(8). Under this rule, a distribution of property will include a distribution of stock by a QOF C corporation to the extent that §301 is applicable, pursuant to §305.

[165] Reg. §1.1400Z2(b)-1(c)(9)(i).

[166] Reg. §1.1400Z2(b)-1(c)(9)(ii).

[167] Reg. §1.1400Z2(b)-1(c)(10)(i).

[168] Reg. §1.1400Z2(b)-1(c)(10)(i)(C).

[169] Reg. §1.1400Z2(b)-1(c)(11)(1)(A). The amount that gives rise to such inclusion event is equal to the fair market value of the shares of the controlled corporation and the boot received by the taxpayer with respect to the qualifying investment.

[170] Reg. §1.1400Z2(b)-1(c)(11)(i)(B). This rule is subject to (i) meeting qualification standards as a QOF under Reg. §1.1400Z2(b)-1(c)(11)(B); (ii) adjustments for boot being distributed to a shareholder; and (iii) a modification of the definition to allow for controlled corporation stock to be treated as qualified opportunity zone stock.

[171] Reg. §1.1400Z2(b)-1(c)(11)(ii).

[172] Reg. §1.1400Z2(b)-1(c)(12).

[173] Reg. §1.1400Z2(b)-1(c)(13).

[174] Reg. §1.1400Z2(b)-1(c)(3)(ii).

[175] Reg. §1.1400Z2(b)-1(c)(15).

[176] Reg. §1.1400Z2(d)-1(a)(3).

[177] Reg. §1.1400Z2(b)-1(d)(1)(i). In other words, the taxpayer's holding period (for purposes of §1400Z-2) begins as of the date of the investment in the QOF, rather than the date that the taxpayer acquired the original (and since disposed of) capital asset.

[178] Reg. §1.1400Z2(b)-1(d)(1)(ii).

[179] Reg. §1.1400Z2(b)-1(d)(1)(iii). This would apply (as a result of death of the grantor) to a grantor trust that became a non-grantor trust, the near or legatee of an estate, or beneficiary of a trust.

[180] Reg. §1.1400Z2(b)-1(d)(2).

[181] Reg. §1.1400Z2(b)-1(d)(2)(iii).

[182] §1400Z-2(b)(2)(A). The statute references that this rule applies to gain included under §1400Z-2(a)(1)(A) which relates to when gain is *not* included in gross income, rather than §1400Z-2(a)(1)(B) which provides when gain is included in income. Nonetheless, the Regulations make clear that this rule will apply to gain inclusion as of the applicable inclusion date.

[183] §1400Z-2(b)(2)(B)(i) and Reg. §1.1400Z2(b)-1(e)(3)(ii).

[184] Reg. §1.1400Z2(b)-1(e)(1).

[185] Interestingly, this rule allows for taxpayers to, in effect, take a loss with respect to its investment at December 31, 2026 even though the taxpayer has not disposed of its investment and the fair market value may in fact increase in value up through the date that investment is sold or exchanged without any tax liability applicable at the time of sale.

[186] Reg. §1.1400Z2(b)-1(c)(8)-(12).

[187] Reg. §1.1400Z2(b)-1(e)(4). Note that it the "lesser of" rule applicable for paragraph (e)(3) which reduces gain inclusion to fair market value also applies to a partnership such that the gain in a fully taxable transaction would be less than the remaining deferred gain.

[188] Note that this rule makes no reference to the partner's share of liabilities under §752. However, since the liabilities are normally held at the partnership level, the extinguishing of such liabilities would take place.

[189] Final Regulations, Summary of Comments and Explanation of Revisions

[190] Reg. §1.1400Z-2(b)-1(g)(4)

[191] Reg. §1.170A-1(c)(2). See also Rev. Rul. 59-60 and Rev. Rul. 83-120. Although Revenue Ruling 59-60 (which describes the valuation of closely held business interests) was issued to value interests for purposes of estate and gift valuations, the ruling has been widely adopted by the valuation community for various tax-related purposes, and general valuation principles for non-tax purposes as well. This ruling details the specific attributes and criteria that should be used to determine the fair market value of such interests (including factors that reduce fair market value, such as lack of control and lack of marketability with respect to such interests).

[192] §1400Z-2(b)(2)(B)(i).

[193] §1400Z-2(b)(2)(B)(ii).

[194] §1400Z-2(b)(2)(B)(iii).

[195] §1400Z-2(b)(2)(B)(iv).

[196] §1400Z-2(c).

[197] Reg. §1.1400Z2(b)-1(g)(1)(i) (first sentence).

[198] Reg. §1.1400Z2(b)-1(g)(1)(i)(second sentence).

[199] Reg. §1.1400Z2(b)-1(g)(1)(ii).

[200] As determined under Reg. §1.1400Z2(b)-1(c)(6)(iii) and Reg. §1.1400Z2(b)-1(c)(7)-(12).

[201] Reg. §1.1400Z2(b)-1(g)(1)(ii)(A)-(B). See Reg. §1.1400Z2(b)-1(g)(3)(i)(C) for an example illustrating the application of this rule.

[202] Reg. §1.1400Z2(b)-1(g)(2).

[203] Reg. §1.1400Z2(b)-1(g)(4).

[204] Reg. §1.1400Z2(b)-1(g)(5).

[205] Reg. §1.1400Z2(b)-1(g)(4)(i); *See e.g.* Reg. §1.1400Z2(b)-1(g)(f)(10-(11).

[206] Reg. §1.1400Z2(b)-1(g)(5)(ii)(B).

[207] Reg. §1.1400Z2(b)-1(h)(1).

[208] As provided in Reg. §1.1400Z2(b)-1(c)(6)(iv) (relating to mixed fund investments) or (c)(7)(iii)(relating to aggregate changes in S corporation equity ownership).

[209] Reg. §1.1400Z2(b)-1(h)(2).

[210] Reg. §1.1400Z2(b)-1(h)(3).

[211] Reg. §1.1400Z2(c)-1(b)(1).

[212] Reg. §1.1400Z2(c)-1(b)(1)(iii).   Note, however, there is no reduction in gain exclusion even if the taxpayer recognized an amount less than the remaining deferred gain under §1400Z-2(b) if the fair market value of the investment was less than the remaining deferred gain.

[213] Reg. §1.1400Z2(c)-1(c).

[214] Reg. §1.1400Z2(c)-1(b)(2).

[215] Reg. §1.1400Z2(c)-1(b)(1)(i).

[216] Since, under the statute, this election applies solely to an investment, a number of issues are present that could potentially disrupt the legislative intent to cause such a sale (in the manner contemplated under the statute) to be tax-free: First, it is not clear whether a liquidation would be treated as a sale or exchange of the qualifying investment.  In many cases, an underlying partnership will sell its assets, distribute the net cash proceeds to its partners, and then liquidate.  Second, if the election is made upon disposition, and the disposition is deemed to occur after final distributions in a liquidation, the step up in basis as a result of the election would be zero.  These concerns are mitigated by the taxpayer-friendly rules of the Regulations.

[217] Reg. §1.1400Z2(c)-1(b)(2).

[218] Reg. §1.1400Z2(c)-1(b)(2)(i). Since this rule is likely to be interpreted as expanding the statutory regime, it is only applicable after the final regulations with respect to §1400Z-2(c) are adopted.  *See* Reg. §1.1400Z2(c)-1(f). This rule was adopted under the Final regulations issue don January 13, 2020.

[219] Reg. §1.1400Z2(c)-1(b)(2)(ii)(A). For the purposes of the Regulation, gain and losses include all gains and losses except for ones that arise from the sale or exchange of any item of inventory, as defined in §1221(a)(1), in the ordinary course of business. Gains from bulk sales of inventory as part of a sale of a business would be eligible for exclusion as they are not defined as sale in the ordinary course of business.

[220] Reg. §1.1400Z2(c)-1(b)(2)(ii)(B)(1).

[221] Reg. §1.1400Z2(c)-1(b)(2)(ii)(B)(1).

[222] *See* Reg. §1.1400Z2(b)-1(c)(6)(iv)(B)

[223] Reg. §1.1400Z2(c)-1(b)(2)(ii)(B)(1).

[224] The Regulation explicitly provide that this does not affect the AAA of an S Corporation and cannot be treated as a disproportionate distribution by an S Corporation.

[225] Reg. §1.1400Z2(c)-1(b)(2)(ii)(B)(2).

[226] Reg. §1.1400Z2(c)-1(b)(2)(ii)(B)(3)(i).

[227] Reg. §1.1400Z2(c)-1(b)(2)(ii)(B)(3)(ii).

[228] Reg. §1.1400Z2(c)-1(b)(2)(ii)(B)(2)(ii)(D)..

[229] Reg. §1.1400Z2(c)-1(b)(2)(ii)(C)(1). Any provision that disallow deduction otherwise allowable under subtitle A for amounts paid or incurred (such as §265) are not applicable.

[230] Reg. §1.1400Z2(c)-1(b)(2)(ii)(C)(2).

[231] Reg. §1.1400Z2(c)-1(e).

[232] Reg. §1.1400Z2(c)-1(e)(2).  The notice must be mailed to the shareholder unless the shareholder has provided the QOF REIT with an email address to be used for such purposes.  Moreover, the QOF REIT must provide the IRS with the data specified by the IRS with respect to the amounts and dates of capital gains dividends designated by the QOF REIT for each shareholder.

[233] Reg. §1.1400Z2(c)-1(e)(3)(i).

[234] Reg. §1.1400Z2(c)-1(e)(3)(ii).

[235] Reg. §1.1400Z2(c)-1(e)(3)(iii).

[236] Reg. §1.1400Z2(c)-1(e)(3)(iv).

[237] Reg. §1.1400Z2(c)-1(e)(4)(i). Note that if a QOF REIT identifies an amount that exceeds the aggregate long term capital gains realized on such sales or exchanges for that taxable year, the designated identification is invalid in its entirety.

[238] Reg. §1.1400Z2(c)-1(e)(4)(ii).

[239] https://www.irs.gov/newsroom/opportunity-zones-frequently-asked-questions. In general for federal income tax purposes, the term partnership or corporation generally refers to any entity that is treated as a corporation or partnership (as the case may be) for federal income tax purposes, which would refer to any entity that is so eligible to be treated as either a corporation or partnership including, without limitation, a general or limited partnership, limited liability company, business trust, real estate investment trust, regulated investment company, etc.

[240] Reg. §1.1400Z2(d)-1(a)(1)(ii)(A). The entity may also be organized under the law of a Federally recognized tribe.

[241] Reg. §1.1400Z2(d)-1(a)(1)(iii).

[242] Reg. §1.1400Z2(d)-1(a)(1)(ii)(B). A U.S. territory includes American Samoa, Guam, the Commonwealth of the Northern Mariana Islands, the Commonwealth of Puerto Rico, the U.S. Virgin Islands, and any other territory not under the jurisdiction of one of the 50 states, an Indian tribal government or the District of Columbia where a QOZ has been designated.

[243] Reg. §1.1400Z2(d)-1(a)(2).

[244] The language included on the draft Form 8996 provided the following: "Check this box only if you are electing to decertify as a QOF. The election to decertify as a QOF is voluntary. If you make this election, you must attach a statement to the Form 8996 making this election along with the date of the election. The election to decertify becomes effective on the first day of the month after the month in which the QOF elects to decertify as a QOF. For example, if an entity elects to decertify on July 1, the decertification becomes effective on August 1."

[245] See e.g., PLR 202206015; PLR 202206016; PLR 202205020; PLR 202205021; PLR 202202009; PLR 202116011; PLR 202103013.

[246] §1400Z-2(d)(1).

[247] Reg. §1.1400Z2(d)-1(a)(2)(i).

[248] Reg. §1.1400Z2(d)-1(a)(2)(ii).

[249] Reg. §1.1400Z2(d)-1(a)(2)(iii). If a QOF fails to identify its first month, the first month of the eligible entity's taxable year will be the first month that taxable year.

[250] Reg. §1.1400Z2(d)-1(a)(2)(iii)(B). If an investor invests in an entity prior to the date it elects to be treated as a QOF, and remains within the 180-day period, to avoid the risk that such investment is not treated as an eligible investment as of the election date, the cash invested should be treated as a loan that is then converted to equity at the time that the entity elects to be treated as a QOF.

[251] IRS Form 8996, Part I. At the time the QOF is organized, it may not have identified or aware of all of the business activities that it will engage in. Under these circumstances, the QOF should carefully choose the language incorporated within its organization documents, which can be achieved through generic or boilerplate terms.

[252] In practice, such language is not included in the state formation documents (and some state forms do not

even permit such language). Thus, including such language in the operating agreement is likely sufficient and meets the purpose requirement of the statute.

[253] Reg. §1.1400Z2(d)-1(a)(1)(iii).

[254] Reg. §1.1400Z2(d)-1(a)(2)(iv)(A).

[255] Reg. §1.1400Z2(d)-1(a)(2)(iv)(A).

[256] Reg. §1.1400Z2(d)-1(a)(2)(iv)(B).

[257] Reg. §1.1400Z(2)(d)-1(b)(1)(i); §1.1400Z(2)(d)-1(b)(2)(i)(A).

[258] Reg. §1.1400Z(2)(d)-1(b)(2)(i)(A).

[259] Reg. §1.1400Z(2)(d)-1(b)(3). The "applicable financial statement" method may only be used if such applicable financial statement (are prepared according to U.S. GAAP) requires, or would otherwise require, an assignment of value to the lease of tangible property.

[260] Reg. §1.1400Z(2)(d)-1(b)(4)(ii)(A). The regulations explicitly provide that for the purpose of the 90-percent, the acquisition of qualified opportunity zone stock or a qualified opportunity zone partnership interest is treated as a purchase of such interest by the QOF.

[261] Reg. §1.1400Z(2)(d)-1(b)(4)(ii)(B).

[262] Reg. §1.1400Z(2)(d)-1(b)(3).

[263] Reg. §1.1400Z(2)(d)-1(b)(4)(iii)(A).

[264] Reg. §1.1400Z(2)(d)-1(b)(4)(iii)(C).

[265] Reg. §1.1400Z(2)(d)-1(b)(4)(iii)(B). The three month rule in §1274(d)(2) does not apply to determine the applicable Federal rate for the purposes of the 90-percent asset test.

[266] Reg. §1.1400Z(2)(d)-1(b)(4)(iii)(D).

[267] Reg. §1.1400Z(2)(d)-1(b)(4)(iii)(D)(1).

[268] Reg. §1.1400Z(2)(d)-1(b)(4)(iii)(D)(2).

[269] Reg. §1.1400Z(2)(d)-1(b)(2)(iii). The test much be applied consistently within a taxable year, but can change year to year.

[270] Reg. §1.1400Z(2)(d)-1(b)(2)(i)(B).

[271] Reg. §1.1400Z(2)(d)-1(b)(2)(i)(C). Since the QOF may choose whether or not to include the recently contributed cash or exclude it, the selection to include or exclude such assets will not bind the QOF in the subsequent testing period.

[272] Reg. §1.1400Z2(f)-1(b).

[273] §1400Z-2(d)(2)(D).

[274] As set forth in Reg. §1.1400Z2(d)-2(b)(1) through (4).

[275] §179(d)(2)(A). For purposes of applying the related party rules under §267 for purposes of this rule, in applying §267(b) and (c), paragraph 4 of §267(c) shall be treated as providing that the family of an individual shall include only his spouse, ancestors and lineal descendants.

[276] Reg. §1.1400Z2(d)-2(b)(1)(i). In addition, the Regulations require that there is no plan or intent to have the seller reacquire the property, otherwise the property will not be treated as QOZBP.

[277] Reg. §1.1400Z2(d)-2(c)(1).

[278] Reg. §1.1400Z2(d)-2(c)(2). There is a presumption that a lease between unrelated parties will be at market rates. Related parties should obtain an appraisal from an independent third party to avoid causing the QOF structuring to fail. If the lease is not bona-fide, such property will not be treated as QOZP and may

cause the QOF or QOZB to fail the investment standard tests.

[279] Within the meaning of Reg. §1.1400Z2(d)-1(c)(3)(iii).

[280] As defined in Reg. §1.1400Z2(d)-1(c)(3)(iv), which is generally the 30 month period beginning on the date that the lessee receives possession of property under the lease and ends the earlier of the date that is 30 months after the date that the lessee received possession, or the last day of the term of the lease.

[281] Reg. §1.1400Z2(d)-2(c)(3).

[282] Note that nonqualified property may be *contributed* (rather than leased) to an opportunity zone so long as, at the end of the working capital safe harbor period, the QOZB will meet the 70-percent tangible property standard. *See* Reg. §1.1400Z2(d)-1(d)(3)(vi)(D). However, the contributor will have a mixed investment resulting in taxable gains at disposition since the qualified investment is based on the adjusted basis of the fair market value, with the excess of fair market value over adjusted basis treated as a non-qualifying investment.

[283] Reg. §1.1400Z2(d)-2(b)(3)(i)(A).

[284] Reg. §1.1400Z2(d)-2(b)(3)(B).

[285] Reg. §1.1400Z2(d)-2(b)(3)(iii)

[286] Reg. §1.1400Z2(d)-2(b)(3)(iv)

[287] Reg. §1.1400Z2(d)-2(b)(3)(v)

[288] Reg. §1.1400Z2(d)-2(b)(3)(i)(C)

[289] Reg. §1.1400Z2(d)-2(b)(3)(ii)

[290] Reg. §1.1400Z2(d)-2(c)(3)

[291] Reg. §1.1400Z2(d)-2(c)(4)

[292] §1400Z-2(d)(2)(D)(i)(III)

[293] §1400Z-2(d)(2)(D)(ii); Reg. §1.1400Z2(d)-2(b)(4)

[294] Reg. §1.1400Z2(d)-2(b)(4)(iv)(A)

[295] Reg. §1.1400Z2(d)-2(b)(4)(B)

[296] This ruling also illustrates, as set forth in the facts, the conversion of a building from industrial use to multi-family residential use is permitted and that a 60% allocation to land and a 40% allocation to building is reasonable under these facts.

[297] Reg. §1.1400Z2(d)-2(b)(4)(E)

[298] Reg. §1.1400Z2(d)-1(d)(3)(vi)(D)(1)

[299] Reg. §1.1400Z2(d)-1(d)(3)(vi)(D). This rule is consistent with Reg. §1.1400Z2(d)-2(b)(4)(ii) which provides that tangible property that is undergoing substantial improvement is treated as satisfying the requirements as QOZBP during the 30-month working capital safe harbor period.

[300] Reg. §1.1400Z2(d)-2(b)(4)(iii).

[301] Reg. §1.1400Z2(d)-2(b)(4)(v).

[302] Reg. §1.1400Z2(d)-2(b)(4)(v)(C).

[303] Reg. §1.1400Z2(d)-2(b)(4)(iv)(A).

[304] Reg. §1.1400Z2(d)-2(b)(4)(iv)(B).

[305] Reg. §1.1400Z2(d)-2(b)(4)(iv)(C).

[306] Reg. §1.1400Z2(d)-2(b)(4)(iv)(D).

[307] Reg. §1.1400Z2(d)-2(b)(4)(iv)(E).

[308] §1400Z-2(d)(2)(D)(i)(III) and Reg. §1.1400Z2(d)-2(d)(1). The Regulations follow the statutory language, requiring that in the case of tangible property that is owned or leased by the QOF, during substantially all of the QOF's holding period for the tangible property, substantially all of the use of the tangible property was in a qualified opportunity zone.

[309] Reg. §1.1400Z2(d)-2(d)(3).

[310] Reg. §1.1400Z2(d)-2(d)(4). This is a very taxpayer friendly result. Under the New Markets Tax Credit program, the "substantially all" threshold is 85%. The QOZ program is more flexible and less likely to cause inadvertent noncompliance.

[311] Reg. §1.1400Z2(d)-1(d)(1).

[312] §162(a).

[313] *Commissioner v. Groetzinger*, 480 U.S. 23 (1987)

[314] *Higgins v. Commissioner*, 312 U.S. 212 (1941). The test in *Higgins* is very fact intensive, as it requires a determination with respect to the course of conduct of the taxpayer to ascertain whether the business-related activity undertaken is sufficient to qualify as a trade or business.

[315] Reg. §1.1400Z2(d)-1(c)(2) provides that if an entity is classified as a corporation for federal tax purposes, then an equity interest in the entity is qualified opportunity zone stock if the criteria below are otherwise satisfied.

[316] §1400Z-2(d)(2)(B)

[317] Reg. §1.1400Z2(d)-1(c)(2)(i)(C) provides that the term "substantially all" – as applied to the QOF's *holding period*, means 90 percent. The Preamble to the Second Proposed Regulations reflects that since "taxpayers are more easily able to control and determine the period for which they hold property" the 90 percent threshold (as compared to the 70 percent threshold utilized for another purposes) is appropriate.

[318] It is not clear whether a subsequent contribution of property (other than cash) to a corporation in a transaction to which §351 applied could cause the QOF to be treated as having acquired the stock of the qualified opportunity zone stock in exchange for property other than cash. If that would be the case, the transactions involving the QOF and the qualified opportunity zone stock should be structured in light of these rules.

[319] Reg. §1.1400Z2(d)-1(c)(2)(ii)(A). This section also notes that even if the purchase occurs after issuance, the stock was never qualified opportunity zone stock.

[320] Reg. §1.1400Z2(d)-1(c)(2)(ii)(B). This section also notes that even if the purchase occurs after issuance, the stock was never qualified opportunity zone stock.

[321] Reg. §1.1400Z2(d)-1(c)(2)(ii)(C)

[322] Reg. §1.1400Z2(d)-1(c)(3) provides that if an entity is classified as a partnership for federal tax purposes, then a capital or profits interest in the entity is qualified opportunity zone partnership interests if the criteria below are otherwise satisfied.

[323] §1400Z-2(d)-1(c)(3)(i)(A)

[324] Reg. §1.1400Z2(d)-1(c)(3) provides that the term "substantially all" – as applied to the QOF's *holding period*, means 90 percent. The Preamble to the Second Proposed Regulations reflects that since "taxpayers are more easily able to control and determine the period for which they hold property" the 90 percent threshold (as compared to the 70-percent threshold utilized for other purposes) is appropriate.

[325] It does not appear (based on the explicit permission that property be contributed to a QOF) that

subsequent contributions of property (other than cash) to a partnership in a transaction to which §721(a) applied would cause the QOF to be treated as having acquired the partnership interest of the qualified opportunity zone stock in exchange for property other than cash.

[326] §1400Z-2(d)(3)(a) and Reg. §1.1400Z2(d)-1(d)(1).

[327] A QOZB may not rely on this rule unless the business property was used by a QOZB in a QOZ for at least two , excluding the period of time that the property was either substantially improved, or was covered by the working capital safe harbor.

[328] Reg. §1.1400Z2(d)-1(d)(2)(i).

[329] Within the meaning of Reg. §1.475(a)-4(h)

[330] Reg. §1.1400Z2(d)-1(b)(1)(ii), 1.1400Z-2(d)-1(b)(2)(ii)(A).

[331] Reg. §1.1400Z2(d)-1(b)(2)(ii)(B). A five percent zone taxpayer is an entity that has self-certified as a QOF and owns a 5% equity interest in the entity. The interest must be at least 5% in voting rights and value.

[332] Reg. §1.1400Z2(d)-1(b)(2)(ii)(B).

[333] Reg. §1.1400Z2(d)-2(d)(4).

[334] Reg. §1.1400Z2(d)-2(d)(4)(iii).

[335] Reg. §1.1400Z2(d)-2(d)(4)(iv).

[336] Reg. §1.1400Z2(d)-2(d)(4)(v).

[337] Reg. §1.1400Z2(d)-1(d)(2)(i)

[338] Reg. §1.1400Z2(d)-1(b)(2)(ii)(A). This rule reflects that a QOF could change the methodology each year to achieve optimal outcomes, although the same methodology must applied consistently in the aggregate for each taxable year (and not asset by asset).

[339] Reg. §1.1400Z2(d)-1(b)(3).

[340] Reg. §1.1400Z2(d)-1(b)(3)(ii).

[341] Reg. §1.1400Z2(d)-1(b)(4)(ii).

[342] Reg. §1.1400Z2(d)-1(b)(4)(iii).

[343] Reg. §1.1400Z2(d)-1(b)(4)(ii)(B).

[344] §1397C(b)(2) (referenced by §1400Z-2(d)(3)(A)(ii)). Reg. §1.1400Z2(d)-1(d)(3)(i).

[345] Reg. §1.1400Z2(d)-1(d)(3)(iii)(A).

[346] Reg. §1.1400Z2(d)-1(d)(3)(iii)(B).

[347] Reg. §1.1400Z2(d)-1(d)(1).

[348] *See Commissioner v. Lincoln Savings & Loan Association*, 403 U.S. 345, 352 (1971).

[349] *See Commissioner v. Heininger*, 320 U.S. 467, 471 (1943).

[350] *Commissioner v. Groetzinger*, 480 U.S. 23 (1987).

[351] *Hazard v. Commissioner*, 7 T.C. 372 (T.C. 1946)

[352] *Schwarcz v. Commissioner*, 24 T.C. 733 (1955).

[353] *Hendrickson v. Commissioner*, 78 T.C.M. 322 (1999).

[354] *C. States, S.E. and S.W. Areas Pension Fund v. Fulkerson*, 238 F.3d 891 (7th Cir. 2001).

[355] *C. States, S.E. and S.W. Pension Fund v. Personnel, Inc.*, 974 F.2d 789 (7th Cir. 1992).

[356] Reg. §1.1400Z2(d)-1(d)(3)(iii)(C)(1) Ex. 1.

[357] Reg. §1.1400Z2(d)-1(d)(3)(iii)(C)(2) Ex. 2.

[358] Reg. §1.1400Z2(d)-1(d)(3)(i)(A).

[359] Reg. §1.1400Z2(d)-1(d)(3)(i)(A)(1) & (2).

[360] Reg. §1.1400Z2(d)-1(d)(3)(i)(A).

[361] Reg. §1.1400Z2(d)-1(d)(3)(i)(B).

[362] Reg. §1.1400Z2(d)-1(d)(3)(i)(B)(1) & (2).

[363] Reg. §1.1400Z2(d)-1(d)(3)(i)(C).

[364] Reg. §1.1400Z2(d)-1(d)(3)(i)(E)(1).

[365] Reg. §1.1400Z2(d)-1(d)(3)(i)(E)(2).

[366] Reg. §1.1400Z2(d)-1(d)(3)(i)(C).

[367] Reg. §1.1400Z2(d)-1(d)(3)(i)(E)(3).

[368] §1397C(b)(4) (referenced by §1400Z-2(d)(3)(A)(ii)). Reg. §1.1400Z2(d)-1(d)(3)(ii)(A).

[369] Reg. §1.1400Z2(d)-1(d)(3)(ii)(A).

[370] Reg. §1.1400Z2(d)-1(d)(3)(ii)(B).

[371] Reg. §1.1400Z2(d)-1(d)(3)(vi)(C).

[372] Reg. §1.1400Z2(d)-1(d)(3)(vii)(C).

[373] §1397C(b)(8) (referenced by §1400Z-2(d)(3)(A)(ii)). Reg. §1.1400Z2(d)-1(d)(3)(iv).

[374] §1397C(e).

[375] Reg. §1.1400Z2(d)-1(d)(3)(v).

[376] Reg. §1.1400Z2(d)-1(d)(3)(v).

[377] Reg. §1.1400Z2(d)-1(d)(3)(v)(A).

[378] Reg. §1.1400Z2(d)-1(d)(3)(v)(B).

[379] Reg. §1.1400Z2(d)-1(d)(3)(v)(C).

[380] Reg. §1.1400Z2(d)-1(d)(3)(v)(E). If the QOZB is located within a federally declared disaster area, the business is granted not more than an additional 24 months to consume its working capital assets as long as it complies with the working capital safe harbor requirements. Reg. §1.1400Z2(d)-1(d)(3)(v)(D).

[381] Reg. §1.1400Z2(d)-1(d)(3)(iv)

[382] Reg. §1.1400Z2(d)-1(d)(3)(vii)(C).

[383] Reg. §1.1400Z2(d)-1(d)(3)(vi)(B).

[384] Reg. §1.1400Z2(d)-1(d)(3)(vi)(C).

[385] Reg. §1.1400Z2(d)-1(d)(3)(v).

[386] Reg. §1.1400Z2(d)-1(d)(3)(vi)(D)(1) and (2). *See* discussion of the application of this rule to nonqualified property discussed in Section 0 (*Treatment of Property During the Working Capital Safe Harbor Period*).

[387] Reg. §1.1400Z2(d)-1(d)(3)(vii)(A)-(D).

[388] Reg. §1.1400Z2(d)-1(d)(3)(vii)(E).

[389] §1400Z-2(d)(3(A)(iii) referring to §144(c)(6)(B). Reg. §1.1400Z2(d)-1(d)(4)(i).

[390] Reg. §1.1400Z2(d)-1(d)(4)(ii)-(iii).

[391] *Opportunity Zone Tax Breaks for Weed Businesses? Mnuchin Says No*, O'Neal, Bloomberg Tax Daily Tax Report, May 16, 2019.

---

392 §1400Z-2(e)(4)(C).

393 Reg. §1.1400Z2(f)-1(c).

394 Reg. §1.1400Z2(f)-1(c).

395 Reg. §1.1400Z2(f)-1(c).

396 Reg. §1.1400Z2(f)-1(c)(3)(i).

397 Reg. §1.1400Z2(f)-1(c)(3)(iv).

398 Reg. §1.1400Z2(f)-1(c)(3)(v). A QOF convert a hog farm to a sheep goat farm and made significant capital improvements to existing farm structures, construction of new structures and installation of new irrigation system.

399 Reg. §1.1400Z2(f)-1(c)(3)(vii).

400 §1400Z-2(f)(1). A QOF, in its first year, cannot be assessed a penalty for a month prior to the entity's first self-certification period Reg. §1.1400Z2(d)-1(a)(2)(iv)(B).

401 §1400Z-2(f)(1).

402 §6621(a)(2).

403 §1400Z-2(f)(2).

404 §1400Z-2(f)(3).

405 Reg. §1.1400Z2(d)-1(d)(6)(i).

406 Reg. §1.1400Z2(d)-1(d)(6)(iii).

407 See §45D.

408 See §47.

409 See §42.

410 See §41.

411 See §48.

412 See §51.

413 See §1400Z-1(e).

414 §45D(c).

415 §45D(a)(2).

416 The details of the NMTC program are beyond the scope of this guide. However, the differences in the structures of the respective programs do not allow for the typical, common structure utilized for QCDEs of making loans in low income communities, requiring an equity investment model to apply. Moreover, the types of investments allowed under the NMTC program are generally more restrictive than under the QOZ program (e.g, residential rental real estate is not a qualifying investment).

417 See §42.

418 Since the credits under the LIHTC program are based on the entity's tax basis in the low-income housing project, clarification by Treasury of the impact on the zero basis rule for a QOF for an LIHTC investment would be helpful to ensure that none of the LIHTC credits are lost due to the zero basis rule in §1400Z-2(b). Presumably, this would not affect the inside basis of the assets, however, without any guidance by Treasury, this point remains uncertain.

419 §47(c)(1)(B).

420 §47(a).

[421] See §1202.

[422] In order to qualify as QSBS, the stock must be held in a C corporation, that conducts an active trade or business (excluding certain types of businesses) and at the time that the stock was issued, the gross assets of the corporation did not exceed $50 million. Thus, this structure is often utilized for venture investments.

[423] Reg. §1.1400Z2(a)-1(b)(12).

[424] Reg. §1.1400Z2(a)-1(b)(13).

[425] Reg. §1.1400Z2(a)-1(b)(14).

[426] Reg. §1.1400Z2(a)-1(b)(15).

[427] Reg. §1.1400Z2(a)-1(b)(16).

[428] §1400Z-2(d)(1).

[429] Reg. §1.1400Z2(a)-1(b)(20).

[430] Reg. §1.1400Z2(a)-1(b)(19).

[431] Reg. §1.1400Z2(a)-1(b)(23).

[432] Reg. §1.1400Z2(a)-1(b)(26).

[433] Reg. §1.1400Z2(a)-1(b)(27).

[434] §1400Z-2(d)(2)(D).

[435] §1400Z-2(d)(2)(C).

[436] §1400Z-2(d)(2)(A).

[437] §1400Z-2(d)(2)(B).

[438] Reg. §1.1400Z2(a)-1(b)(34).

Made in the USA
Middletown, DE
21 August 2023

37083249R00124